Pocket guide to
Trading online

Pocket guide to
Trading online

Put your money where your mouse is

Alpesh B. Patel

FINANCIAL TIMES
Prentice Hall

An imprint of **Pearson Education**
London / New York / San Francisco / Toronto / Sydney / Tokyo / Singapore
Hong Kong / Cape Town / Madrid / Paris / Milan / Munich / Amsterdam

PEARSON EDUCATION LIMITED

Head Office:
Edinburgh Gate
Harlow CM20 2JE
Tel: +44 (0)1279 623623
Fax: +44 (0)1279 431059

London Office:
128 Long Acre
London WC2E 9AN
Tel: +44 (0)20 7447 2000
Fax: +44 (0)20 7240 5771
Website: www.financialminds.com

First published in Great Britain in 2001

The right of Alpesh B. Patel to be identified as Author
of this Work has been asserted by him in accordance
with the Copyright, Designs and Patents Act 1988.

ISBN 0 273 65635 X

British Library Cataloguing in Publication Data
A CIP catalogue record for this book can be obtained from the British Library.

This publication is designed to provide accurate and authoritative information
in regard to the subject matter covered. It is sold with the understanding
that neither the authors nor the publisher is engaged in rendering legal,
investing, or any other professional service. If legal advice or other expert
assistance is required, the service of a competent professional person should
be sought. The publisher and contributors make no representation, express
or implied, with regard to the accuracy of the information contained in this
book and cannot accept any responsibility or liability for any errors or
omissions that it may contain.

10 9 8 7 6 5 4 3 2 1

Designed by Sue Lamble
Typeset by Northern Phototypesetting Co. Ltd, Bolton
Printed and bound in Great Britain by Bath Press Ltd, Bath

The Publishers' policy is to use paper manufactured from sustainable forests.

To Mummy, Ramilaben B Patel

Just in case I never told you how special you are to me.
Your sacrifices drive me.

About the author

Trading

Alpesh started buying stocks 18 years ago at the age of 12, moving on from privatization stocks to penny shares. Today he concentrates on US and UK stocks as well as futures and options trading, making extensive use of the internet for research since he was a Congressional Intern in 1994 and combining this with his own technical analysis systems. On Channel 4's latest 'Show Me The Money' series he came number 1 of 45 expert stock pickers.

Alpesh is a graduate in the Joint Honours School of Philosophy, Politics and Economics from St. Anne's College, Oxford and has a degree in law from King's College, London. He is a fellow of Corpus Christi College, Oxford, researching e-learning strategies for marketing financial services. As a pupil barrister, Alpesh was involved in advising banks, building societies and pension funds on financial services. He left the bar to trade full time and founded TraderMind Ltd.

The company has acted as consultant up to CEO level of multi-billion dollar online trading companies advising on market entry and expansion strategy, site content and design. TraderMind's customers include some of the leading UK online financial companies.

Currently, Alpesh is a co-founding director of several UK, European, Indian and Latin American technology companies specializing in financial portal development, specialist financial software creation, online trading content provision on and offline, execution-only and advisory brokerage services (Pathburner.com) and application service provision. He has been appointed by LIFFE (the world's third largest derivatives exchange) as Commentator on Stock Futures.

Alpesh is also the co-founder of SreeSharada – a UK/Indian joint venture IT company offering specialist financial applications to global online trading and financial portals and presently working with Pearson Education to establish an 'e-books' joint venture with Indian software partners.

TV, radio and print

Alpesh also writes the 'Diary of an Internet Trader' for the weekend *Financial Times*. He appears weekly on 'Bloomberg Money on the Net' and each week interviews senior executives of internet companies on '@Bloomberg'.

Channel 4 recently described Alpesh as the UK's best known internet trader. He has been interviewed on CNN, Sky Business News, CNBC, Bloomberg TV, Channel 4, the Money Channel, BBC World Service, BBC TV and BBC Radio 4 and 5 as well as weekly by phone on numerous US radio shows syndicated in all 50 states to discuss internet issues with audiences to up to 7m. He has also been profiled in *Asian Age*, *The Times of India*, *FT.com*, *Hindustan Times* and the *Independent* and quoted in *Bottom Line* (circulation > 1m), *Tornado-Insider*, *India Today* and the *Guardian* among others. He has been a regular on ITV's 'Tonight with Trevor McDonald' (5m viewers) and appeared on the 'Money Programme' which reaches a potential 100m viewers through BBC World.

Books

Alpesh is the author of *Net Trading* (FT.com 2000), *Trading Online* (FT.com 2000), *The Mind of a Trader* (FT Pitman 1998). *Net Trading* has been translated into Spanish and German and *Trading Online* is an international bestseller translated into German, Spanish and French, with translation options held by Chinese, Danish, Russian, Italian and Polish publishers. The French title is the *Les Echo Guide to Trading Online*.

Trading Online was the number one best-selling investment book on Amazon UK and reached number two on the overall bestseller list. It was listed as one of the top ten investment books of 1999 in the *Independent* and top ten business books of 1999 by Amazon UK and BOL.co.uk

Lectures

Alpesh regularly speaks on online trading, trading psychology and technical analysis around the world.

alpeshpatel@tradermind.com

Contents

Acknowledgements / xi

Introduction / xiii

1   **Trading online is easy and trading online is difficult:** know what you are getting into / 1

2   **Getting going:** opening accounts and all that jazz / 9
    Appendix: essential hardware and software / 22

3   **Getting trading ideas:** screens and filters / 31

4   **On trading systems:** online traders do it in front of a PC / 35

5   **Charts, technical analysis and momentum indicators** / 47

6   **The anatomy of a price rise and strategy rules** / 75

7   **Fundamentals** / 83

8   **More fundamentals:** this time – earnings / 103

9   **The trade planned** / 115

10 **Money and risk management for e-trading** / 125

11 **Eyes and ears open:** monitoring / 143

12 **Essential trading psychology for online trading** / 147
    Appendix: something new, something exciting: universal stock futures / 161

13   **Top trading psychology tips from leading traders of the world** / 181

14   **Chats and boards** / 187

15   **Speeding things up** / 193

Appendix 1: Quotes sites / 197

Appendix 2: Earnings sites / 202

Appendix 3: Fundamental data / 205

Appendix 4: Brokers / 208

Appendix 5: Technical analysis sites / 223

Glossary / 231

Acknowledgements

Thanks to Jonathan Agbenyega who moved so quickly on the book from our first conversation that the second conversation we had was whether I had finished the book yet. If only all companies moved so fast.

Poor Amanda Thompson who had to chase me for the manuscript – sorry and thanks.

Thank you, Jamie Landale, for planting the germ of the idea, and being so enthusiastic and loaded with ideas, that I insist you should have a scribe following you around to write down everything.

Then there's the whole team at FTPH – once again a superlative effort. I hope I don't become high maintenance – at least not until we sell a million copies.

Introduction

Perhaps it is because I placed my first trade at the age of 12, to try to earn enough money to avoid a paper round, or perhaps because I could safely be described as an internet geek (freak could be equally applicable) that I am so fanatical about online trading.

It is this fanaticism that makes me wonder why even more people do not want to trade online? I don't mean widows and orphans, but people who already have share brokerage accounts with traditional brokers. Perhaps I can explode some concerns they and even those who do trade online may have.

Why you need to read this book

To avoid being overwhelmed by the information, you need clear, simple action plans to quickly find the type of information *you* need, and then manage it effectively for profit. The competitive advantage that the internet offers will be rapidly eroded without such an efficient professional approach.

This book provide the necessary approach and framework needed to trade as profitably as possible on the internet.

By the end of the book you will have a professional approach which you can refer to each time you want to trade, and know which sites to visit for precisely the type of information you want.

The book contains all the essentials for trading online, from an expert who is used to explaining all the important issues to novices and advanced traders alike.

You are definitely not alone

BROKERAGE COMMISSIONS TO TOP $5.3 BILLION		
Online Trading Forecast		
	1998	2002
Commission Revenues	$1.3 billion	$5.3 billion
Accounts	6.4 million	24.7 million
Individual Investors	5.6 million	22.7 million
Percent of Total Investors	8%	30%
SOURCE: INTERNATIONAL DATA CORP.		

For those worried that such an activity may be a little risky for its
'frontier-type' nature, you are definitely not going to one of a few
online traders trying out untested technology. According to IDC,
there were 6.4 million online broker accounts in the USA alone as
far back as end of 1998 and there will be 24.7 million by the end of
2002.

In Europe online trading is going to have an exponential
increase. According to JP by 2002 there will be some 8 million
people trading online in Europe. The message must be – there is
going to be a mad rush, join in or be left out.

Online trading accounts in Europe

1997	1999	2002
Under 100,000	900,000	Over 8 million

I don't do that kind of thing

Of course online trading is not for everyone. But a common
misconception is that you have to trade short term to justify
opening an online account. Wrong! Even if you only buy shares
once a year, you could save in commission charges.

Start small

What size is your average trade?

You need not be put off from opening an online account by the false belief that you should shift your entire holdings to your online account. In the UK and USA it appears that most online traders are being quite shrewd and trading online with a small amount of the overall capital they have devoted to trading and investing.

In the USA, according to one recent survey most people trade online with less than $10,000 in their accounts. In the UK, the Association of Private Client Investment Managers and Stockbrokers found that the average online trade was for £4,730. So, there is nothing to stop you testing the online brokerage waters with a small amount of capital.

Truly global

And online trading is truly global. You can buy Sony and China Telecom stock in dollars as easily as Coca-Cola and IBM. In September and October 2001 I travelled to Miami, London, Beijing, Kuala Lumpur and Puerto Rico – everywhere I have been able to trade and everywhere I have met online traders.

If you have a bank account, you should have an online trading account.

Alpesh B Patel

1

Trading online is easy and trading online is difficult:
know what you are getting into

- Should I increase my involvement in online trading?
- Exactly what are the pitfalls that never seem to be discussed?
- How can I go in, eyes wide open?

Online trading is habitually portrayed as a very simple way to make money. It is not. I know from experience that what the market gives easily with one hand, it takes away with both hands, twice as much, and a lot more readily.

I know from experience, and from the ample e-mails I receive each week of online trading newbies who double their money in a week or a month, only to lose five times as much in a year, that online trading is a difficult but rewarding skill. In this chapter I want to get across the pitfalls as well as the joys, so that everyone enters the online trading revolution fully aware of and equipped to face both the difficulties and the joys.

> *I want to get across the pitfalls as well as the joys, so that everyone enters the online trading revolution fully aware*

Online trading is easy

Do not fall foul of any of the following assertions. They may come from an advertisement, or a friend or even an overheard conversation:

- **False:** Online trading is the way the few who dare make a fortune.

- **True:** There is no more a secret to online trading than there is in buying books from Amazon or buying a second-hand kidney from Ebay. The mechanics are relatively easy, but knowing what to buy and when, and then when to sell is where the skill lies. Whether you are an online trader or not, you will need to master the skills of investment and this book tries to teach you those.

- **False:** The costs you save in placing an order online make it far easier to come out ahead at the end of the year.

- **True:** Discount online brokers do offer very low brokerage rates, saving you a lot of money compared to placing trades with a full-fee broker. But you still need to be good at picking stocks.

- **False:** Online trading allows rapid short-term gains.

- **True:** While with online trading you can trade relatively short term because orders are transmitted electronically, most online brokers are not intended to be used as a substitute to your being a floor trader. They confirm your orders as quickly as possible, but

TABLE 1.1 ■ Brokerage commisions to top $5.3 billion

Online trading forecast		
	1998	2002
Commission Revenues	$1.3 billion	$5.3 billion
Accounts	6.4 million	24.7 million
Individual Investors	5.6 million	22.7 million
Percent of Total Investors	8%	30%

Source: International Data Corp.

day trading, where you are looking to buy and sell in a few seconds, is not appropriate through online brokers, because by the time you get a price, place the order, get a confirmation, review the new price, place a new order, get another confirmation, the market could have moved away from what you thought it was.

> **False:** *Online trading offers an instant daily income from a small capital start-up*

That small move matters to day traders because even 1/32 of a dollar is a big hit to them. Online brokers are not for that type of trading. However, if you are looking to hold for at least a day or longer they are ideal.

- **False:** Online trading offers an instant daily income from a small capital start-up.

- **True:** We have all heard stories of the online trader who makes $150 daily and therefore a comfortable living over a year. The more you want to make, the more capital you need. If you are looking to make money every day, then you will have to trade every day. That will be expensive in commissions, let alone time, and soon you may find yourself without any trading capital. That is why most short-term traders look to place, say, two trades a week instead.

- **False:** There is so much free information about stocks on the internet that you have an advantage over everyone else in making profitable trades.

- **True:** Information without an understanding of how to use it, or what it means, is useless. There is a lot of information in a law library, yet the librarian is not a lawyer, let alone a good one. Again, I want to provide, with the help of other online traders who have placed comments on bulletin boards, more than just information, but knowledge, and wisdom too. I will show you what I consider the best places to get information, but that is just the starting point.

> **True:** *Information without an understanding of how to use it, or what it means, is useless*

We must then know what to do with it to make money, and that is where I have tried to cram in the pages of this book the accumulated knowledge of many profitable strategies of our fellow online traders.

■ **False:** You can make profits off the back of more knowledgeable traders' postings on chat sites and bulletin boards.

■ **True:** The best places for research are reputable sources of company information such as Hoover's (US) or Hemmington Scott (UK). Chat rooms are a great place to ask questions, double-check your own views, but they are not a place to form opinions about a stock, because any old anonymous Joe or Josephine can type away at the keyboard promoting stocks of interest only to them. (For more details on chat rooms and bulletin boards see Chapter 14.)

Chat rooms are a great place to ask questions, double-check your own views, but they are not a place to form opinions about a stock

---

 expert advice

Arthur Levitt, Chairman SEC

From a statement of 27.2.1999
While the manner in which orders are executed may be changing, the time-honoured principles of evaluating a stock have not. An investor's consideration of the fundamentals of a company – net earnings, P/E ratios, the products or services offered by the company – should never lose their underlying importance.

Investing in the stock market – however you do it and however easy it may be – will always entail risk. I would be very concerned if investors allow the ease with which they can make trades to shortcut or bypass the three golden rules for all investors:

1 Know *what* you are buying.

2 Know the *ground rules* for all investors under which you buy and sell a stock or bond.

3 Know the level of *risk* you are undertaking.

Online investors should remember that it is just as easy to lose money through the click of a button as it is to make it, if not easier:

- **False:** You can give up your day job and work from home.
- **True:** While some people have given up careers to pursue online trading (myself included) it requires capital and experience. Without capital you will not earn enough to pay the bills, and without the experience, you will make mistakes that the pressure to perform intensifies.

Also, giving up the day job is a risky proposition for anyone. Do you really want to sit all day in front of the computer, by yourself? Even if you make money, how fulfilling would a 20 percent pay rise be, if the quality of life is tedious? So, be mentally prepared if you do want to go down that route, and do not start online trading with a view to leaving full-time employment – that may not be the right thing to do.

> *False: You can give up your day job and work from home*

Customer best practice

There are key things every online trader should do to avoid the problems of trading on the internet.

Keep accounts

The more often you trade, the more confirmations you will receive. You must keep all these in a safe place, and I recommend keeping a file on a spreadsheet which provides a running list of purchases, sales, profits, losses, commissions paid.

> *You should know immediately how much you are paying in commissions and what kinds of profits or losses you are making*

This way, you should know immediately how much you are paying in commissions and what kinds of profits or losses you are making. If you also note how many days you are keeping your positions open, you may notice, for instance, that there is a link between how long you keep a position open and the profit or loss from it.

I found, years ago on one system, that the longer I kept a position open the less I was making on it. That suggested to me that I may not have been cutting my losses short or my system may lose its predictive power after a short time from a buy signal or any other number of reasons. But I knew to investigate further.

All this may seem a far cry from the 'making money hand over fist' visions you may have had, but while online trading is fun, it is also hard work if you want to do it seriously.

Question, question, and then, question some more

Always question advice and try to find independent corroborating advice. If there is someone talking up a stock, only ever use that to start your own research. Discount the advice itself.

Contingency plans

You should be fully aware of your options for placing a trade if you cannot gain access to your account online. A good major reputable broker will always be able to offer telephone back-up in case of a failure of technology. They may also have a fax number or touch-tone phone trading. It may be that you only need to access this once a year, if at all, but do make a note of the methods. There is no point planning to go online to find the appropriate information, if it is not available because the site is 'down'.

Cancelled?

If you cancel an online trade, you must make sure you get confirmation of the cancellation, before assuming it was cancelled. (Almost sounds like a country and western song – maybe not then.) Otherwise, you may place other orders in the erroneous belief that your previous trade was cancelled. Sometimes it is too late to cancel a trade because it is impossible to get to the floor broker in time.

Take care with your clicking ways

When executing the order you must always be careful not to click away like crazy on the 'place order' button just because you do not get instantaneous feedback. Otherwise, you may well end up owning more of Microsoft than Bill Gates does.

Trading on margin

Some brokers allow trading on margin through margin accounts. This is where they borrow money from the broker to trade. The amount they can borrow depends on the firm itself. The loan is secured on the securities and cash belonging to the client held with the broker.

➤ *example*

If a customer has $50,000 cash in an account, the firm requires a deposit margin of 50%, in which case the customer may borrow $50,000 and so buy $100,000 of stock. If the price of the security falls so that the next day it is worth only $60,000, since the customer still, of course, owes $50,000, his equity is only $10,000.

If the maintenance margin for the account is 25% then the client has to maintain $15,000 in equity (if he has $60,000 in stock) and the client here has only $10,000, so he will get a margin call of $5000, in which case, if he did not meet the call, the broker could liquidate stock to meet that margin call without additional authority from the customer.

When trading on margin do not forget you are increasing the risk you face, because you could end up having to pay back more than you have in assets. Always remember you are borrowing money to buy stocks and remember you do not have to trade on margin.

Summary

Online trading deserves our respect or it will have our money. Frankly, I will give it respect – it's a lot cheaper. You cannot appreciate enough that there is more to online trading than placing an order. It is a mechanism. You still need to do your homework – albeit

✳ *Online trading deserves our respect or it will have our money* with the quantity and quality of information on the internet, doing your homework is easier than ever and can possibly even be fun. You need, too, to be aware of boring things like margin requirements, broker back-up phone numbers, record keeping – dull but essential.

2

Getting going:
opening accounts and all that jazz

- Okay, how do I go about opening an account then?
- What do all those terms mean anyway?
- What's the good hardware to have – have I got it?
- What about the software that gives me the edge?

Setting up

Can I open an account?

Um, let me think. Sure you can – but it can depend on which country you're a resident in. For example, a US citizen may not be able to open an account with a UK online broker. But don't worry, the e-broker's account-opening process will make all that clear.

Also you'll almost always need to be over 18 and have a bank account. Most brokers allow you to set up an account online in minutes. There are usually no set-up charges and no requirement for a minimum balance either. But note that some brokers don't yet allow a joint account.

What sort of account do I need? There are different types.

Cash account

The simplest form of account. A minimum opening balance is commonly required. You can only trade if you have the cash in your account. No credit is given and you'll have to maintain a balance (sometimes termed the 'equity balance') to keep your account alive. This needn't always be as much as the opening balance though. Some brokers may charge you if you don't trade for a certain period.

Margin account

Essentially a credit facility enabling you to trade without necessarily having all the cash in your account. A proportion of the price is usually needed, but the rest comes from a loan – with interest. The loan will be from the broker or one of its affiliates so it might not always be the most competitive.

A margin account lets you make a secured loan against your own portfolio. The advantage is that you do not have to sell any of your portfolio to obtain the cash. Furthermore, you have no repayment schedule.

> *A margin account lets you make a secured loan against your own portfolio*

Not all brokers offer this facility. Those that do will do all the calculations for you in terms of how much you can borrow to invest. Lending you money is after all in their interest – it means you will trade more and pay more commissions. Of course it could also mean that if a blindingly great opportunity comes your way, you don't have to wonder where you'll get the cash.

- You are free to repay the loan at any time, unless your collateral falls below the required amount.
- While most investors use the borrowed cash to buy additional securities, you can use it for any purpose.

- However, the wholly owned securities in your portfolio are collateral for the loan.

- You will also need a margin account if you are engaging in short sales.

- It's only really for the more experienced trader and not the beginner, as the risk is that you can lose your money a lot quicker.

Short account

A short sale involves selling securities that you don't actually own with the intent of buying them back at a lower price. It takes quite a sophisticated kind of broker to offer this facility – many brokers won't have them.

How do I set it up?

Typically, you can be up and running in minutes by completing a simple online registration form on the broker's site. Have your bank details to hand and follow the on-screen instructions (see Diagram 2.1).

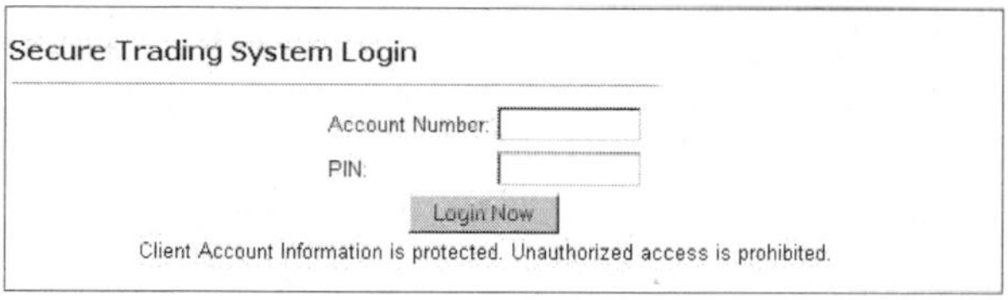

Secure Trading System Login

Account Number: [   ]

PIN: [   ]

[Login Now]

Client Account Information is protected. Unauthorized access is prohibited.

DIAGRAM 2.1 ■ Typical login screen

Do I need special hardware or software?

No. Anyone with an internet connection can trade online. Having said that, make sure to read the appendix to this chapter, just in case you have an unusual system.

You should try and ensure you have the latest Microsoft Internet Explorer (www.microsoft.com) or Netscape Navigator (www.netscape.com). These days most internet service providers (ISPs) provide a secure connection. If in doubt verify with your ISP's customer support people.

One of the advantages of an online broker is that you don't have to access your account from the same PC – you can trade anywhere, anytime – because you would just go to the broker's website and login with your username and password which you would be given when you open the account. There I go, getting carried away again.

Trading

How do I start trading?

Once you've opened an account and logged on you'll need to put money into your account before you can start trading – what a pity! Now you just have to decide what to buy.

What are the stages for placing a trade online? Brokers vary but typically you'll need to give the following information:

1 Account number and PIN (personal identification number) – your PIN will often be sent separately under plain cover, like a credit card PIN.

2 Your ID – the name you registered in. (Sometimes called username etc. – you get the idea.)

3 Action required – buy, sell, sell short, buy to cover etc.

4 Order size – number of shares.

5 Type of order – market price, limit, stop, stop limit.

6 Price – if order is a limit, stop or stop limit.

7 Duration – how long offer is to continue (e.g. good for the day offers lapse at close of the day's trading).

Do I have to place orders on-screen?

It makes sense to use the on-screen facility if you're keen to maximize the efficiency of online trading, but there may be times when this isn't so desirable. Brokers acknowledge this

> **It makes sense to use the on-screen facility if you're keen to maximize the efficiency of online trading**

and often offer different methods of placing orders (see Diagram 2.2). In addition to on-screen ordering you'll commonly be able to place orders by touch-tone telephone, by fax or even – for those big, complex orders – by speaking directly to a broker.

However, if it isn't placed online, then it usually costs a little more.

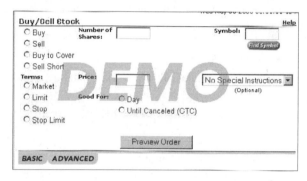

DIAGRAM 2.2 ■ An order screen

What sort of stocks can I buy?

Most brokers will let you buy the stocks on just about all, except perhaps the more esoteric, exchanges of the country you are in. In the US that means NYSE, NASDAQ stocks, of course, plus usually more. In other words, don't worry, you'll have loads to choose from.

What price do I trade at?

You trade at the real-time price, that is, the price offered in the marketplace. But bear in mind that many of the research tools provided to you by your broker will be delayed by 15 minutes. So you're buying at the true price but using slightly old analysis. If the research is delayed it will tell you nearby.

How long does it all take?

How long do you want it to take? Assuming you have money in your account and know what you want to buy, you can commence trading right away. If the stock market is open and you want to buy at market price, your order will be executed immediately. (See later section for information about after-hours trading.)

However, during busy periods you may not be able to access the broker's site, or if you do, your order may not reach them through the internet immediately. In other words, there can sometimes be delays. With most major reputable brokers, this should not happen.

Is there any advice about what to buy?

At the end of the day it's your call – you have to make a decision on what to buy. But most brokers offer research and analytical tools to help you make an informed decision. Typically, a brokerage site will enable you to view a graph of the price and other trading history of a particular stock (see Diagram 2.3). You should also be able to get news updates about a specific company and compare its performance against other similar companies.

Also, by reading this book, you'll be better able to understand what all those tools can do for you and make better decisions.

How easy is it to sell?

This will vary according to the particular broker you've registered with. Generally, you'll simply have to log on in the prescribed way – entering your id and password is typically what's called for – then click onto the trading page and select the shares you wish to sell. There will usually be clear, step-by-step instructions on the screen (see Diagram 2.4).

What's a nominee account?

Sometimes you'll find that your broker refers to a nominee account. This is simply a means of facilitating the rapid

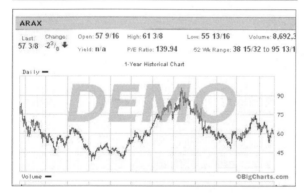

News Headlines

»

INTERVIEW-Vietnam, China, can't hold back Internet-AOL
Reuters, 04/24/2000 07:18

INTERVIEW-Vietnam, China, can't hold back Internet-AOL
Reuters, 04/24/2000 07:18

RESEARCH ALERT - TMP Worldwide reinstated
Reuters, 04/24/2000 07:13

Edgix Appoints Mike Young to Lead Global Network Operations; Edgix Strengthens
Management Team with Seasoned Executive from UUNet
Business Wire, 04/24/2000 06:48

NYSE INDICATION LAST 60 2/8 BID 56 ASK 59
Reuters, 04/24/2000 06:42

Be Free and Webs Unlimited Announce Channel Cash; First Affiliate Marketing Add-
In for Microsoft FrontPage 2000
Business Wire, 04/24/2000 06:26

ARAX

Last: 57 3/8   Change: -2³/₈ ↓   Open: 57 9/16   High: 61 3/8   Low: 55 13/16   Volume: 8,692,3
              Yield: n/a   P/E Ratio: 139.94   52 Wk Range: 38 15/32 to 95 13/1

1-Year Historical Chart

Daily ▬

90
75
60
45

Volume ▬   ©BigCharts.com

DIAGRAM 2.3 ■ Brokers give ample information for an informed decision

Symbol	Last	Change	View
DJIA	10434.92	-6.98	Summary
S&P 500	1244.94	-0.92	Summary
NASDAQ	2254.98	-7.53	Most Actives
AMEX	899.33	3.25	Most Actives
NYSE	624.73	1.73	Most Actives

Market Snapshot   Refresh

my Account

View:
- Balances   - Transactions
- Positions   - Review
- Electronic   Orders
  Statements

DIAGRAM 2.4 ■ Typical market overview screen

processing of each trade. The broker holds your shares in a pooled nominee account. You remain beneficially entitled to your shares (i.e. you still 'own' them) but the nominee account allows the broker to process your trade immediately, rather than waiting for the formal legal certificates to be completed. It's like the system used by banks to process your money and hold it for you – it keeps administrative costs down without undermining your ownership of the shares.

Can I access my account any time?

Yes, most brokers permit access round the clock, seven days a week, all year (see Diagram 2.5).

Balances		Help
	Current Balances	Start of Day Balances
Buying Power	2,797.44	2,797.44
Available Funds	1,398.72	1,398.72
Cash Balance	0.00	0.00
Margin Balance	-182.53	-182.53
Equity Balance	2,350.27	2,350.27
Equity Percentage	93.00%	93.00%
- Long Value	2,532.80	2,532.80
- Short Value	0.00	0.00
Total Maintenance Requirement	801.87	801.87
Liquidation Value	2,353.27	2,353.27

Start of Day - Account balances are based on the previous market close.
Current - Account balances are adjusted by the most recent activity. Open orders are not included in this calculation.
Balance amounts are subject to change.

DIAGRAM 2.5 ■ Check the status of your account 24/7

What about evenings and weekends?

Although you can access your account and place trades any time, trades will only be executed when the stock exchange is open.

Beware: Trades placed outside opening times will be executed at the price when the market next opens – this may vary from the price at the time you place the trade. For this reason, you'll find that brokers will usually ask you to set a limit order for every out of hours trade placed.

So I just place my order and go?

Not quite, there are a number of different types of order. You have to decide which you prefer.

Types of order

After you have decided whether you plan to buy or sell a stock, the typical order ticket will give you a few more choices. You can choose between a market order, a limit order, a stop order and a stop limit order. Each of these choices has its own implications as seen in the following.

It sounds complicated, but most people start with market orders, then, as they become more confident, move to the others. Soon you'll be talking stop limit order placement like an old pro.

A market order is an instruction to buy or sell a stock at the best market price available at the moment. For example, you may want to buy 100 shares of XYZ stock. If the current market for XYZ is 50 bid and 50 1/8 ask, you may or may not get the stock at 50 1/8.

Market orders will definitely be filled, but you cannot be sure of the price. Prices will vary with current conditions and these conditions are not always reflected on your computer screen. The actual price at which your order is filled may be better or worse than you expected.

A limit order lets you place a price restriction on your transaction. You indicate that you are only willing to buy or sell a stock at a certain price or better. Your order is not filled unless the stock trades at that level. Placing a limit order, however, is not a guarantee that your trade will be executed at your limit price. It does, however, eliminate the risk that your order will be filled at a price worse than you expected.

For example, if you want to buy CrazyGuy stock at $80 a share once again, and the market price is 80 bid and 80 1/8 offer, your order cannot be filled immediately. If somebody comes to sell the stock at $80, then your order will be filled if it is next in line for execution. If more buyers enter the pit and drive up the stock price, your order will not be filled.

A stop order is an order to buy or sell a stock at the market price once the price reaches or passes through a specified point, called the 'stop price'. This type of order is generally used by people who own a stock and want to make sure they sell out if the stock price starts to drop. The stop price placed on a sell stop order must be below the current bid price of the security.

For example, if you buy 100 shares of Maniac Driver at $50 a share and you want to protect yourself from a potential loss, then you might place a stop order. If you placed a stop order at $45 a share, the moment Maniac Driver traded at $45, your order would become live and the broker or specialist would sell it to the highest bidder. Stop orders in volatile issues will not guarantee an execution at or near the stop price. Once triggered, they are competing with other incoming market orders.

Stop orders can be placed for buy orders as well. The stop price specified for a buy order must be above the current asking price.

A stop limit order performs like a stop order with one major exception. Once the order is activated (by the stock trading at or 'through' the stop price), it does not become a market order. Instead, it becomes a limit order with a limit price equal to the former stop price.

For example, you place a stop limit order to sell stock with a stop price of $45 a share. As with the stop order, once the stock trades at $45, your order is triggered. However, the broker cannot sell it below $45 a share no matter what happens (see Table 2.1).

The advantage of this order is that you set a minimum price at which your order can be filled. The disadvantage is that your

TABLE 2.1 ■ What can happen to your stock

	Market	Limit	Stop	Stop limit
Description of fill	Filled at best price available when order reaches the market	May be filled when the stock trades at the limit price you set	Will be filled at best price available in the market after the stock trades at your stop price	Will be filled at the stop price, if possible, after the order is activated

order may not be filled in certain fast market conditions. In this case, if the stock keeps moving down, you will keep losing money.

Fill or kill (FOK) is an instruction either to fill the entire order at the limit price given or better or cancel it.

How do I know if my trade has gone through?

You should always receive on-screen confirmation of executed trades in your secure area. Trades placed with a limit attached, either in or out of market hours, will also appear on the screen as pending. On top of online confirmation, you should also receive a formal contract (often by e-mail).

What if I make a mistake when placing an order?

It's not in anybody's interests to let you make an erroneous trade. Online brokers usually require you to confirm the details of your trade at least once – more often than not, twice. But there's only so much an automated brokerage system can do to protect you, so make a mistake twice and you will have entered into a contract on that basis – so be careful.

Using your account

How do I get money into my account?

The standard ways of transferring money are just as applicable to online trading accounts: debit card payment, bank transfer and cheques. But note you can only use a debit card or direct debit once the transaction has been confirmed.

Your broker may not offer all of these. But one thing is for sure – they want your money, so they will have lots of easy explanations on how to transfer money into the account.

How do I extract money from my account?

You can get money out of your account at any time up to the cleared funds balance in your cash account. Just nominate a destination bank – usually the one given when you registered with the broker. Many brokers don't charge for transfers – but give yourself three working days at least for the transfer to be effected.

How can I close my account?

Not usually a problem. Ensure that you notify the broker in writing – remembering to keep a copy of your letter. Your remaining shares will be transferred to your nominated broker or in paper form. The latter will often attract a handling fee.

Can I keep track of what my stocks are worth?

Simple – your broker will provide a means of clicking straight into your portfolio so that you can keep tabs on your holdings. To view your up-to-the-minute share dealings some sites require you to re-enter your password and id.

Can I move my existing holdings of shares into my account?

Your broker will have an online explanation of how to do this. Usually it is the broker to whom you are transferring who will try to do most of the work for you once you give them your details online and confirm you want to transfer to them.

How do I withdraw my shares from my account?

You can withdraw shares from your nominee account by making a request to your broker. This can be online or in person via your broker's customer services team if you need a little more assistance. Again, transfer in paper form will usually attract a fee.

How will dividend payments be handled?

You'll receive any dividends accruing to your shares straight into your cash account. All tax vouchers relating to dividend receipt will be collected by your broker and forwarded to you annually for the tax year.

What if I am a foreign resident?

Many e-brokers service foreign accounts. However, due to the fact that overseas mail delivery is not conducive to meeting a 3-day settlement, they often require funds or securities to be in the account prior to placing orders.

Charges and interest rates

What will I be charged per trade?

Online brokerages are not always known for the clarity of their pricing schedules. A good way of selecting an online broker is to choose one with a simple pricing structure. A good broker might, for example, keep things to a simple charge of, say, $10 per trade plus a quarterly management fee.

Some brokers are more competitive, such as Ameritrade, at $8 per online trade. But note that you may be charged more for touch-tone or direct broker access trades. Brokers will typically charge you an additional fee on limit, stop and stop limit orders.

How will interest rates be calculated?

When your money is sitting in your nominee account you'd expect it to be accruing interest wouldn't you? Every broker will differ slightly but, in my experience, rates are always similar except for special offers.

Summary

Opening an account really is not that difficult. Remember it is in the interests of the e-brokers to make it as easy as possible for you. It can be fiddly, but take your time and you'll be fine. Trust me. Or just call up their customer services number as you go through the form.

Essential hardware and software

You can't skydive without a plane and you can't trade online unless you *are* online. In this appendix, we look at the minimum hardware a trader needs for trading. You could, of course, go higher spec: that's up to you.

Objective

- Find out what gear is necessary to get up and running as an online trader.

Hardware

Computer

A PC and not a Mac is recommended

For reasons best known to Bill Gates and Steve Jobs, most trading software is not Mac compatible. It makes far more sense, therefore, for you to stick with a PC (which are always Windows compatible) than buy a Mac and be disappointed.

You may have strong views on this already. Sure, it sounds like the VHS/Betamax showdown of folklore. People will tell you one's better than the other; that it's a case of what you get used to; even that Mac, as urban myth has it of Betamax, is the superior machine, unjustly suppressed by big corporate interests. Whatever. The critical issue for the online trader is compatibility.

For trading, even a classic 266 MHz Pentium processor is sufficient

Most entry-level PCs have fast enough processing speeds to undertake all trading tasks. Speed becomes a problem only if you have very many applications open simultaneously and are also playing Doom while trading.

It is not necessary to buy the latest PC

It will go out of date and you will be paying a premium. Instead, buy a cheaper PC and upgrade later.

32 MB RAM (random access memory) is minimum requirement

RAM is the temporary memory in which your computer runs programs, a little like room to play. The more room the computer has, the quicker it can get things done. However, 64 MB is more than enough. If you want you can buy more, but you do not strictly need it for your trading.

3 GB hard drive or larger is best

The hard drive is where all the programs and other things you save are stored. Storage space is useful as over the years we all tend to collect clutter, such as bric-a-brac, spouses, etc. A 3GB drive would probably last most traders until they decide to upgrade their computers (and their spouses).

Windows 2000 operating system is recommended

When it comes to programming trading software, most programmers use the latest version of Windows. The problem with Windows 98 is that it crashes more often than a crash-test dummy. Windows 2000 is based on the industry-standard, 'hard as a rock' Windows NT, which is far more difficult to crash.

CD drive useful, x16 or faster

Most programs and much data are provided on compact disks. A 16-speed one is more than adequate although many computers now come with nothing slower than 32-speed. DVD players are not needed as yet.

Soundcard and speakers

Soundcard and speakers can be useful for online news broadcasts and some trading software, such as metastocks using videos of advisors. However, they are not essential.

Many internet sites provide live broadcasts, and a soundcard and speakers will add even more value to the internet. Fortunately, these are normally thrown in with new computers or are available pretty cheaply.

Modem

Internal or external makes little difference

It does not matter from a trading point of view whether the modem is some electronic wizardry inside the computer or a separate attachment outside it. The latter option may be better if you are not keen on opening up the computer.

At least a 56k modem is recommended

You do not want to be waiting all day to receive trading news and information. The speed of your modem is important to ensure you can have an outside life, too.

Consider ISDN or ADSL/cable broadband if you can afford it or get it

These offer digital connection that is faster than a normal modem. They are lightning fast, but can be expensive.

Cable

About 25 times faster than a dial-up modem. It uses the standard cable tv connection. The only problem is that it's a shared line, so the more people online, the slower the connection. This is just like dial-up modems today, only faster. Despite this, it still looks like being the best home option. Availability is limited at present. Check with your local cable provider.

ADSL (sometimes called DSL)

Asynchronous digital subscriber line is a service provided by some local phone companies. ADSL transmits compressed digital data down part of your standard phone line. The advantage over a modem is that you can still make and receive calls on your phone while being online. Okay, 'so get a second line' you might say; true, but ADSL is also impressive, being similar to cable (i.e. 25 times the speed of a modem).

ISDN

You may well have heard of the intergrated service digital network. It's not as advanced as ADSL, but can be up to twice as fast as a 56.6k modem. Consider it if you can afford the extra cost and cannot get ADSL or cable.

T-1 lines

What most businesses have. Pretty much instantaneous connections with high-capacity data lines.

T-3 lines

Very expensive – i.e. what very big businesses have. Currently unavailable for home use but, as ever, it must surely only be a matter of time ...

Satellite

Currently about seven times the speed of a 56.6k modem. The problem is that you'll need both a dish to receive data and a satellite service provider by phone line in order to send e-mail. Only really worth considering if you have no cable or local digital services such as ADSL or ISDN.

Monitor

17" preferred – twin flat panels even better

Beyond 15" and monitors start getting very pricey. Less than 15" and you start needing a magnifying glass. With 17" screens becoming standard, you could even go to 19".

I have three flat panel monitors which not only save on desk space but also increase productivity since I can monitor share prices on one screen and research on the other two. Speak to your computer vendor about these. Dell, for instance, is particularly good in my experience (wwwdell.com). You can't, of course, just buy a separate monitor and plonk it on. You need a graphics card and preferably 64 or 128Mb RAM.

Anti-glare and anti-radiation filter essential

The radiation emitted from the trading screen that is on all day may cause you to grow a second head, but there is no evidence that two brains would improve your trading performance. So buy a filter and keep your uni-head good looks.

Most modern flat panels would not require such filters.

Printer

Laser printer most expensive but best for drawing charts

These printers have dropped dramatically in price and are best when it comes to printing out all those trading charts and for reading text.

Inkjet minimum requirement

If the purse strings are tight, an inkjet is likely to be adequate for printing charts and text.

Internet service providers (ISPs) and access providers (IAPs)

Choosing an internet service provider (ISP)

Asking an online trader what 'ISP' stands for is a bit like asking a journalist what BBC means. But although many people will have heard of ISPs not everyone will know what it means and, more importantly, what it does. An internet service provider provides access to the web from a pc using your modem (see earlier).

Who?

Well-known ISPs are AOL (America OnLine), Freeserve, Microsoft Network, Virgin and Btclick. They're a bit like your phone company but instead of providing you with a line they give you an entrance into the web – a doorway, if you like. The major ISPs offer a vast range of information and web links to their subscribers including search tools or 'engines' as they're usually known.

Don't worry about finding an ISP – the biggest (e.g. AOL) will find you. If you've just bought a new PC, you'll probably find two or three ISPs ready loaded onto your hard drive. ISPs differ as to what they offer and how much they charge. If you went for the ADSL or IDSN option outlined earlier, you'll have been given an ISP connection automatically

Don't worry about finding an ISP – the biggest (e.g. AOL) will find you

If you don't have your desired ISP already on your PC, you'll have to get hold of their dial-up software. These are mostly free usually free with PC magazine CD give-aways or as a free mailing. Once you've found the software, follow the instructions that come with it. Alternatively, you can sign up to another ISP if you're already online – but this gets a little 'chicken and egg' so I'm assuming you're not already online. Once you've downloaded the software and signed up with the ISP, you're ready to go online – or 'surf' as your dad no doubt insists on calling it.

Things to remember:

1 *Over-subscription*: Try out the ISP before you subscribe. If it's slow it may be because there are too many subscribers for the ISPs servers to handle. This is particularly so at peak times like midday and early evening. Try out the service at different times of the day.

2 Do they allow you to have more than one member per account? You may find this useful for family use.

3 If you use a laptop and travel, how accessible is the ISP globally?

An unlimited online time plan is required

ISPs and IAPs usually have different charging plans, many charging by the number of hours spent using their services. Since we traders may spend a lot of time online, the cheapest pricing option is almost always the 'unlimited' time plan, since there is only a monthly flat fee for access.

Take a free trial

Try before you buy is the advice here. Almost all ISPs and IAPs permit a one-month free trial and it is best to use this to test their reliability.

Browsers

The latest version of Internet Explorer or Netscape Navigator is recommended

If you are looking for a browser then you want the most sophisticated one and one catered for by almost all internet sites. So Internet Explorer and Netscape Navigator are highly recommended. They are available free from cover CDs of most internet magazines.

Make sure you regularly check for upgrades and consider having the 'add-ons' when you download the software – all those bells and whistles and sometimes used by trading sites (www.microsoft.com; www.netscape.com).

Bookmarks

It is essential to familiarize yourself with Bookmarks in Netscape Navigator or Favorites in Internet Explorer for the purposes of managing information.

PC TV

If you are trading from home, then you could have a TV playing in a small section of your monitor, such as CNBC or Bloomberg, to keep you up to date with the markets. Not essential, but I like it, also great for watching the Simpsons while you write books – only kidding: you, the reader, have my undivided attenti ...

Summary

This appendix has covered the basics for those already familiar with computers and the internet. Most entry-level PCs will accommodate all the aspects mentioned here and you will not have much to worry about. People with older systems may need to upgrade, however.

3

Getting trading ideas:
screens and filters

Don't be scared to feel you don't know anything, because you don't know anything until you learn.

Brian Winterflood, Managing Director, Winterflood Securities

In this chapter

In this chapter we cut to the chase. We want to generate trading ideas and so we start with filters, screens and lists.

Objectives

- Find out how to use the best online filter sites for trading ideas.
- Make the most of tips on screening for stocks.

How people choose what to buy: some popular methods

Most people, whatever they trade, have several tried and tested methods they use to conjure the inspiration in deciding what to purchase.

Filters, screens and lists

So many stocks, so little time. That is where stock filters and screening sites come in handy. They all work on similar criteria and that is why I have grouped them all together. For instance with some you can enter certain criteria you want stocks to match, e.g. earnings per share under 30 and revenue growth above 25 percent and the filter returns a list of stocks matching your criteria.

So many stocks, so little time

They are a very quick and useful way of getting trading ideas because the computer does most of the hard work for you.

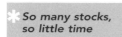

example

A typical stock screen

When screening or filtering for stocks (Diagram 3.1) you may decide that you want a company with strong earnings likely to keep a cash reserve (through paying low dividends) which it may use to return value to shareholders by share buy-backs or acquisitions or mergers, in which case you may look for a stock with the following characteristics:

1 a three-year historical earnings growth rate of 20 percent or more

2 a return on equity (ROE) of 25 percent or more

3 stocks providing annualized total returns over the past five years of 20 percent or more companies with payout ratios (dividends as a percentage of earnings) of 15 percent or less and dividend yields (dividends as a percentage of stock price) of 1 percent or less.

What would you get? Well, one of the companies listed was Intel. You could then undertake further research.

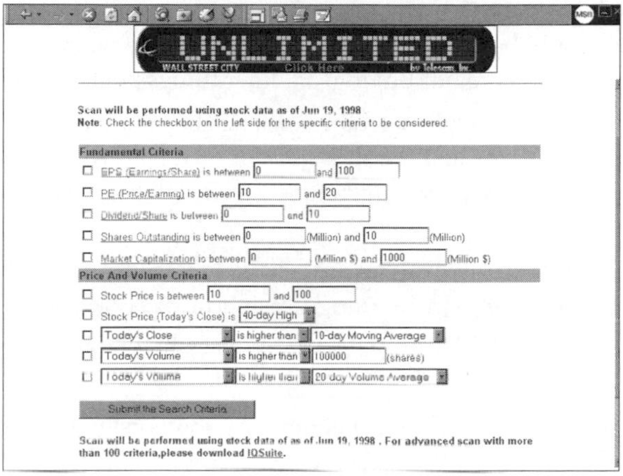

DIAGRAM 3.1 ■ Stock prospecting using a screen

How do you know what criteria to use?

Most good sites will have some pre-programmed filters already incorporated that will fill in the gaps for you. For instance, if you click on 'growth criteria' a set of values may get filled into the screening boxes. You could then leave them as they are or add your own. Other common searches have such names as in the following list. (I have included in brackets a summary of why we would want to look at stock lists generated by those screens or filters):

> *Most good sites will have some pre programmed filters already incorporated that will fill in the gaps for you*

- high earnings growth stocks (strong earnings should translate into strong stockprice growth)

- lowest p/e ratio stocks (low stock price to earnings should mean the price of the stock rises to reflect the earnings generated)

- attractive gross margin stocks (the greater the profit margin, presumably, the greater the profits, which in turn should reflect in increased stock prices)

- high sales growth (sales are the input for earnings, which in turn affect the stock price)

- high insider buying (if the company's directors are buying then the stock should be a good purchase relative to one where the company insiders are not buying, all other things being equal)

- strong stocks recently weak (if the stock has been having a strong run except for just the short term then it may well present an opportunity to buy it cheap before it resumes its longer term strong trend)

- undervalued (those stocks that are relatively low in price and so should rise, relative to the earnings, cash flow or book value they hold, when compared to the other stocks in the same industry).

The sites explain the rationale behind why someone would want to do such a search. Other sites will provide lists based on pre-programmed criteria allowing no user changes to those criteria. You would still get a list of stocks and then continue from there with the type of further research we are going to talk about. You can easily spend hours playing around with these prospecting for some gems – and indeed finding them.

Since many sites include filters, I have gone for the sites I consider the most useful, hidden gems on the web, with the most 'bells and whistles'. See the appendices for lists of sites.

Summary

I have tried to provide you with a detailed method of how to get stock ideas from the top filter sites. The tips I offer are based on years of experience and if you make any money from this you can send me a cheque c/o my publishers.

4

On trading systems:
online traders do it in front
of a PC

With proper strategy the strongest enemy may be overcome.

The Mahabharat

The general who wins a battle makes calculations in his temple before the battle is fought. The general who loses a battle makes but few calculations beforehand. Thus, do many calculations lead to victory, and few calculations to defeat.

Sun Tzu, *The Art of War* (edited by James Clavell)

Online trader problems

- Why exactly are online traders using systems and what do they mean by 'system'?
- Should I create my own or take someone else's?
- How do I choose between the wealth of ideas to trade by?
- What am I going to put in my system?
- How do I select the right time frame?

- What do professional traders and private online traders have to advise about systems?

- What are the problems of over-optimization?

Having a trading system is as essential to profitable trading as having a steering wheel is to driving around a corner. Yet you would be surprised by the number of people who try to undertake trading without a detailed understanding of systems. In this chapter we examine some of the issues every good trader faces when making choices about trading systems.

Trading systems 101: Watchya doing here then?

> *Creating a system should be fun, otherwise you should question whether you will enjoy any aspect of trading*

Most online traders, and certainly the good ones, do not trade by the seat of their pants. They do not get their ideas by telepathy about when to buy and when to sell. Instead, they have a 'system'. Many people bandy the word 'system' about without truly having a trading system or without having one as good as it could be.

They just do not actually understand what a trading system really is. So, I thought I would spell it out:

1 A trading system tends to be mechanical in nature in that you input price data and it outputs buy and sell signals, based on rules, although there are good discretionary systems whereby an ultimate decision is made by the trader. For example: 'Buy if today's high price is greater than yesterday's high price by 2 percent on 10 percent greater volume.'

2 A system is built up of an indicator or indicators, such as the relative strength index (RSI). It can have one indicator or a multitude overlaid. For example: 'Buy if the RSI, MACD, and momentum indicators all move above 30.'

3 A good system should be as clear as possible in telling you when

to enter and when to exit the market. Otherwise, the mind being as it is, you will seize on any ambiguity and fail to act according to your trading system.

4 A good system will also incorporate entry and exit strategies (such as using stop losses, limit orders).

5 A good system will also cover issues of risk and money management, such as the amount of total equity to be placed on any one trade, under what circumstances scaling back will occur, etc.

6 A system is not a system until it is back-tested for profitability and then refined and optimized. Until then it is just a speculation.

7 A mechanical, as opposed to discretionary, system is one that is always followed and not overridden on whim. Later, we will compare the two types and examine why online traders prefer each type.

8 Creating a system should be fun, otherwise you should question whether you will enjoy any aspect of trading (or question whether you are congenitally miserable).

System and strategy

A trading system is a complete set of rules relating to every aspect of your trading from entry, position, size, to exit. A strategy is part of a system. For instance, you may have a strategy whereby you only exit on a sell signal from the RSI signal if the price makes a lower low relative to the preceding day. Strategies are part of a system. I thought I would clear that up because we are going to use those two words a lot in this book.

My place or yours?

A common problem online traders face, one they share with other traders, is whether to even bother trying to develop their own trading systems, use someone else's or buy one for several thousand dollars.

There are several key reasons why you should try to develop your own trading system:

■ When you go through all the steps of trying to build your own trading system, even a very simple one, you will learn a lot about trading, such as why it is difficult to make money in the markets, how the market changes over time, how the line between profit and loss can be very fine. Plus a lot more. Education about how prices and indicators interact and how prices move adds to your databank of experience. Of course, you can just give up, go for a drink instead and forget the markets.

■ If you follow someone else's system you are likely never truly to believe in it, especially if it starts making losses. Then you may dump it and waste your money.

■ Another way to lose your money is to buy a system that promises eternal profits, especially on historical tests. Yes, it may be the bee's knees of systems, but what do *you* think?

> *If you follow someone else's system you are likely never truly to believe in it, especially if it starts making losses*

■ You will gain an insight into trading which should result in a perception shift and an understanding that trading is about probabilities not certainties.

Mechanical or discretionary?

Many online traders ask if they should have a purely mechanical trading system or a discretionary one. A mechanical system is one in which, by a strict set of rules, for every market eventuality, you know whether to be in or out of the market. For instance, a very simple system may involve being long if the price is above the 50-day moving average and being out if it is not.

Discretionary system

■ No amount of programming can incorporate human experience into a mechanical system.

■ Can never be as thoroughly back-tested because the trader himself cannot put himself back in time to decide how he would have felt about a particular trade and whether he would have placed it.

■ Do not need to know how to program trading software.

Mechanical system

■ No emotions involved in decision making. Should lead to a less stressful life.

■ Since it can be mathematically back-tested you can have a fairly good idea, albeit inconclusive, about future performance.

■ No constant decision making. Relatively stress free.

With a discretionary system the ultimate decision is down to the trader who may consider all the facts before him plus gut instinct and try to incorporate experience, etc. So, which should you go for? (See Table 4.1.)

There are certain personality-related issues to resolve too, before you decide the type of strategy you should go for. Here is a simple test. It meets the highest standards in psychometric

TABLE 4.1 ■ Discretionary system or mechanical system?

Discretionary system	Mechanical system
No amount of programming can incorporate human experience into a mechanical system	No emotions involved in decision making. Should lead to a less stressful life
Can never be as thoroughly back-tested because the trader himself cannot put himself back in time to decide how he would have felt about a particular trade and whether he would have placed it	Since it can be mathematically back-tested you can have a fairly good idea, albeit inconclusive, about future performance
Do not need to know how to program trading software	No constant decision making Relatively stress free

testing and has been designed with cunning subtlety – so you should take it very seriously.

How disciplined are you when it comes to executing trades?

1 My name is General Colin Powell
2 Very disciplined, always take a signal, no problems
3 Sometimes disciplined, but occasionally go for a wild shot
4 Not very disciplined at all, trade on whim
5 My name is Homer Simpson

Are you mathematical in nature?

1 I've lost count of my age
2 Hate math
3 Intermediate, competent
4 Very good
5 I work for NASA

Do you like programming computers?

1 I can't program the microwave
2 I could probably learn but wouldn't really enjoy it
3 I wouldn't be bad
4 I could do it and would enjoy it
5 I taught Bill Gates all he knows

Are you more logical or more emotional?

1 I cried through *Star Wars*
2 Pretty emotional and feeling based rather than strictly rational
3 Probably a bit of both most of the time
4 I think things through clearly and methodically, logic is my light
5 My name is Spock, I work on the Starship *Enterprise*

What do you enjoy about trading?

1 Soros comes to me for my opinion on the markets
2 I like being involved, part of the game, plus want to profit, too
3 I want to make money, but want to enjoy trading, too

4 I want to make lots of money. Period. I don't care too much about the trading
5 Greed

What type of trader do you admire most?

1 George Soros
2 The type that has to make choices and work hard
3 I don't know
4 The type that can put his feet up
5 John Merriwether

How good are you at decision making?

1 I told you, my name is General Colin Powell
2 Quite good. I like to make them, stick by them and watch them succeed or fail
3 Alright most of the time. Have difficulties occasionally
4 Pretty indecisive
5 I have just spent an hour on this question

How lazy are you?

1 I don't do sleep
2 Not very, I like to work hard, play hard
3 As much as the next guy. I like my short cuts
4 If there is a quicker way of doing something I would like to know it
5 I am answering this in bed. It is 4pm

How do you handle stress?

1 I am a space shuttle commander when I am not sailing naked down the Amazon coated in honey
2 Quite well. It gives me a buzz
3 Sometimes I dislike it
4 Hate it
5 On my wedding night I had to use Viagra. I was 22

Now tot up your scores and use the following guidelines to determine whether you are more suited to a mechanical system or a discretionary one:

9–23 You would handle a discretionary system well given your personality, and would probably enjoy it too

24–36 You could probably handle both quite well. You may want a very mechanical system with occasional override discretion

37+ Better do it by the book. Mechanization for you, my friend, is the best option

Smart, new, and sexy – your very own system: You just gotta have one

Since this is a book about trading systems, I feel obliged to give you a few reasons why you should have one. Although it is arguable that if you have bought the book, you do not need converting.

Trading valium: a stress reliever

Trading gets frustrating. Whoever you are. It gets stressful if you have had a string of losses. It can consume your waking hours and your sleeping ones. You can get to a stage where you think of nothing but how you have been trading. With a trading system some of that stress can be alleviated, if not avoided altogether, if you have the knowledge that your system was tested for profits and that despite some losses you will make money by following it.

> * *While a plan cannot predict the future, it can lay down how you will react to the possible outcomes*

Much anxiety in trading, as in life, stems from uncertainty about the future. It is when we do not know what the future holds that we become anxious. Man, and woman, desires certainty. While a plan cannot predict the future, it can lay down how you will react to the possible outcomes. This is why a plan is essential. It is a list of strategic responses to events beyond your control. You control the only thing you *can* control – yourself.

 *expert advice*

Pat Arbor, former Chairman, Chicago Board of Trade

As a trader you must decide what you are. You are either a speculator, spreader, or local scalper. You have to fit into one of those categories. Me, I am suited to spreading. To find what suits his personality, he just has to see whether or not he makes money at what he's doing. I have had people come into the office saying 'I am a great trader'. I say, 'You're right'. They say, 'Know how to trade'. I say again 'You're right' and they say, 'I predicted that the market was going to go up or down', and I say again, 'You are right. But the bottom line is whether you make any money'.

Consequently, a system removes much uncertainty, which itself is the cause of anxiety, confusion, anger and frustration. A good plan should therefore release psychological energy that is unnecessarily being expended on uncertainties. The flip side is that trading should become effortless, you should be more relaxed and possibly even enjoy your trading more!

Don't chase me

Strategically, too, a good plan improves trading. It assists in identifying opportunities and so stops you from chasing the market. It tells you when to exit, so you are not left clinging to the mast of a sinking ship. You gain some control instead of being swept and buffeted around.

Save me from temptation

A system makes it easier for you to resist the temptation of doing

A plan is a means of changing your trading behaviour for the better

what is comfortable, because in trading, doing what is comfortable is often the wrong thing. Think of how many times you have let a loss run or cut a profit short because it was the comfortable thing to do.

Eventually, as you get used to following your system, it will become second nature. So, too, a plan is a means of changing your trading behaviour for the better. A kind of trading straitjacket, protecting you against your wilder emotions.

 expert advice

Phil Flyn, Vice President, Alaron Trading

If you go into a trade with a wishy-washy attitude, then you are going to be wishy-washy in execution. That is why some plan is better than no plan. You have to look at it like this: win or lose this is a good trade because if I was stopped out when I was wrong, then this is still a good trade. You never make a bad trade. The only bad trade is when you do not follow your rules and you get yourself into trouble. If you look at it from a longer term viewpoint it makes it a lot easier.

I am in charge

Your own trading strategy is going to give you the independence to test your own ideas and not to have to wait for a particular market guru to give you his opinion. The buck can stop with you, for profits and losses.

Pick and choose

When you are building your own trading system, you can pick and choose which fits your trading personality and preferences instead of choosing someone else's system, designed for their particular foibles. For example, you may want a profitable system, but with very few losing trades. You may be happier with such a system than one which is 10 percent more profitable but has double the number of losing trades.

Confidence

With your own creation, you know you have tested it for profitability. That can mean a lot when it comes to actually 'pulling the trigger', when you are unsure whether or not to place a particular trade. Good traders have confidence in their abilities to the point they know they are destined to make money. Part of this confidence comes from having spent hours developing their own systems. Once they execute the trade, confident in the system, they can focus on the trade itself and not have to waste time on whether it was a mistake, or whether 'expert' Joe Shmoe in the newspaper was right in his opinion about the trade.

Emotions are out, certainty is in

For many online traders deciding when to place a trade and when to get out can be an agonizing time. With a system, you can almost automate the process. The additional benefit of this is that you can remove the fear of cutting a loss and the hope that comes from hanging onto losers when you should have cut them.

System is friend, me is enemy

You are your own worst enemy when it comes to trading. You are human, and inevitably make irrational decisions based on tips, fear, greed. The system is like a port in a storm. It keeps you safe and makes sure you remain on track and do not get sidetracked.

(i) *expert advice*

The benefits of a trading system

■ A stress reliever.

■ Prevents market chasing.

■ Controls inappropriate, ill-planned trades.

■ Control over your own trading.

■ Having a made-to-measure system suited to your preferences.

■ Gives you confidence in your trading future.

■ More certainty, less emotion.

5

Charts, technical analysis and momentum indicators

October. This is one of the peculiarly dangerous months to speculate in stocks. The others are July, January, September, April, November, May, March, June, December, August and February.

Mark Twain

In this chapter

Using technical analysis (price charts and indicators) is probably the quickest and easiest way to evaluate the short-term prospects of a stock. If you do it well you can scan through lots of stocks and get a good idea not only of what to buy and when, but of when to sell. For those new to technical analysis (TA), we go through the basics before we go to the killer sites and see how to use them to generate profitable trading ideas.

Objectives

- What is this thing 'technical analysis' people keep talking about?
- Key things we need to know about TA to get trading ideas.

- Using the hidden gems that lie behind the top TA sites in order to get profitable trading ideas.

- Knowing which securities to buy.

- Even if I know what to buy, when is the best time to buy it, so I reduce the chances of the stock going down right after I have bought it?

- What are the signs that a security is 'tanking', i.e. ripe for a fall?

- I can't be bothered reading a load of accounts, analysts' reports and dull stuff like that before deciding what to buy: what should I do?

- How do the big institutions use technical analysis?

Technical analysis

Vast books have been written on TA, so this is a refresher chapter for people who may need reminding of some of the key concepts of technical analysis, but it is also for all those newbies who need to get up to speed about TA.

I am not going to go through every single analytic method known to man and beast. I am going to focus on the techniques I use, those that are the most popular and those the major institutions use. There will be no discussion of the latest esoteric method developed by some overgrown maths professor out of Lima who swears that TA, mixed with a bit of sunspot gazing, produces great trading results. No. You only get the good stuff here.

> **TA is simply a way of trying to find out when to buy low and sell high**

I love TA and, trust me, this stuff is so straightforward once you get the hang of it. I have explained it to Oxford professors and 14-year-old students. Remember throughout that TA is simply a way of trying to find out when to buy low and sell high.

The rationale for technical analysis

To repeat, the reason for using TA is to know when to buy low and sell high. It tends to work best over a time frame of a few days to a few weeks, so is ideal for short-term trading. Many of the indicators and methods of analysis we will examine are trying to determine when traders may have overreacted and have sold too much stock too quickly or vice versa, therefore affording us the opportunity to enter or exit the market at the best time to maximize profits.

But TA does not always work. Nothing in the markets always works – as far I know, although I understand that George Soros may have a better idea than most of what often works. Whenever we use TA, or any other form of analysis, we are in fact looking for points where there is an increased probability of a price move. Let us then look at some tools to determine high-probability price move areas.

Charting

Let us start at the beginning, as simply as possible. The first thing all technical analysts will do is put up a price chart. There are many, many types. Check out for instance Diagrams 5.1, 5.2 and 5.3.

DIAGRAM 5.1 ■ Bar chart

DIAGRAM 5.2 ■ Japanese candlesticks

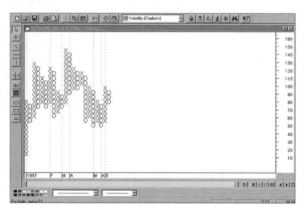

DIAGRAM 5.3 ■ Point and figure chart

Bar charts are the most popular ways of depicting prices. The length is determined by the extremities of the high and the low. The horizontal line on the left of each vertical line represents the opening price and the horizontal line on the right represents the close.

In Japanese candlesticks there is a 'body' and a line (like a wick). The body is a rectangle drawn between the open and close of the day. It is shaded black if the close is lower than the open and white if the close is above the open. The wick is added to join the high and low of the day. Of course, if there is no price movement after the open then there will be no body or wick and just a horizontal line.

I won't bore you with point and figure charts, or for that matter renko or kagi – bar charts and candlesticks are by far the most popular and all we need to know before we undertake a PhD in TA.

Trendlines

A trendline simply joins a series of higher lows or lower highs. Uh? Look at Diagram 5.4. We see the line joining higher lows. Drawing trendlines is best treated as an art and you should not look for exact points, but get a feel for where prices are hitting the approximate narrow area around the line and then moving back up. What trendlines try to represent are areas where there is a relatively increased probability of a price move off the trendline.

You would not trade off the trendline, but rather use it as one piece of evidence when determining likely price moves – more of how to do this later.

DIAGRAM 5.4 ■ Trendlines

Support and resistance

You will often have read or heard something like: 'Prices met stiff resistance today and could not break through the 60 barrier.' By drawing support and resistance levels we are again trying to determine areas where prices are probably, but not certainly, going to behave in a particular way. See for instance Diagrams 5.5 and 5.6. They depict support and resistance levels respectively.

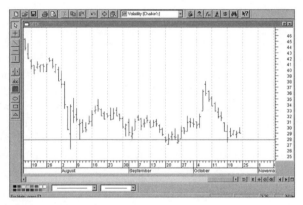

DIAGRAM 5.5 ■ Support

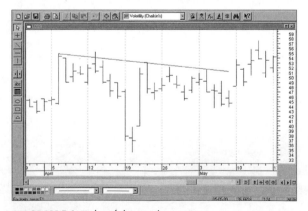

DIAGRAM 5.6 ■ La résistance!

So, when the price approaches the resistance area it has greater difficulty getting past that area and you may decide you want to exit your position (if you are holding one) at that point.

Like trendlines, they must not be thought of as set in stone. They are liable to move and can be penetrated intra-day or maybe even over a couple of days. They should perhaps be thought of as zones of probable price action. In a moment we will look at how to use this actually to trade.

With trendlines and supports and resistances, the probability of a price move in a particular direction increases the longer the trendline has been in 'force', i.e. not penetrated but merely had the price touch it and then bounce off it.

So if a trendline has six points over a six-month period where the price did not pass through it but instead touched and moved in the opposite direction, that will be a strong signal that the price will do this on the seventh approach. Have a look at Diagram 5.7 which should remove the clouds of foggy ambiguity from your mind.

> **With supports and resistances what we are seeing is a battle between buyers and sellers**

With supports and resistances what we are seeing is a battle between buyers and sellers. For instance, at a resistance level sellers may have decided they will start selling a security at that level because it is

DIAGRAM 5.7 ■ Trendlines

overpriced and buyers are too few to do much about it. So the price has to retreat as selling increases.

If the buyers increase in number and size at the crucial point (i.e. go for a push through the line of resistance with reinforcements) then the price may break through with the force of a broken dam, with maurauding buyers pushing the price up higher and short sellers who had not anticipated the breakthrough now having to buy back their positions to limit their losses, thereby becoming buyers and pushing the prices even higher.

This is one reason why the price often jumps at breakouts with a sharp rise, a gap up in price and increased volume. Watch for these things and you will soon get a feel for price action around supports and resistances.

Support and resistance trading strategies

One strategy traders use with, say, resistances is to wait to see if the resistance is broken and, if it is, then – on the basis that all those people who did not expect it to be broken would be wrong and now have to go with the side of the break – prices should break through resistances and, when they do break through, with a significant rise. So, first look for a penetration or breakthrough of the resistance; if there is one, then it should be followed by a big move (i.e. a breakout).

> *So, first look for a penetration or breakthrough of the resistance; if there is one, then it should be followed by a big move*

So what counts for penetration? Given market volatility you could get prices piercing a trendline or support or resistance but then closing back above it. For this reason some technical analysts only draw trendlines and support and resistance levels based on closing prices, because intra-day prices are too erratic to mean a real penetration has occurred. Others say the price must close for two or three days in a penetrating position. (I hope you are not reading this chapter in bed: there is a danger your concentration may be distracted.)

An alternative method of trading is to wait and see if the trendline is not broken and then to trade in the direction of the rebound.

Role reversal

When a support or resistance level is broken it tends then to reverse its role and to become a resistance level or support level respectively (see Diagram 5.8). This is a common occurrence and the same rules about resistances and supports apply as before.

DIAGRAM 5.8 ■ Move trends

Trendlines and supports and resistances can be drawn on any time frame, whether the charts you are using are three-minute or weekly ones. You would first determine the time frame you intend to trade in and choose the bar charts appropriate to that. For instance, if you intend to hold a position for only a few days then you would use the daily charts.

> *Trendlines and supports and resistances can be drawn on any time frame*

Pullback

After the breakthrough of a support or resistance the price will often 'pull back' to the trendline it just broke through (Diagram 5.9). You have to be careful of this because you may think the move has ended, in which case you may exit an otherwise profitable trade prematurely. Unfortunately, you will not know if it is a pullback (which could also be used as another opportunity to enter the trade if you missed it first time) or a false breakout until it is too late.

So the key is to set stop losses and watch the prices like a hawk. If the price breaks through and then pulls back to near the support line again, is it now starting to go back through the support line and continuing on as if it had never broken through (i.e. a false breakout) or is it starting to return in the direction of the breakout? Feel free to take a break, look at the charts, think it over, have a snooze and return to this.

DIAGRAM 5.9 ■ Pullback

Reversal pattern strategies

Reversal patterns are chart patterns which historically have tended to precede a reversal in prices. Again, they are added to our overall evidence of what the price may do, which then gives us a better idea whether we should exit a position or enter one. So let's do a rundown. If you like what you see then you should definitely learn more before trading by picking up some technical analysis books and looking at TA in more detail.

Head and shoulders strategies

An anatomical pattern, this. Have a look at Diagram 5.10 for a nice example. It is not always as clear cut.

This is a common pattern on bar charts and is fairly reliable. The horizontal line represents the 'neckline' and you must always wait

DIAGRAM 5.10 ■ Head and shoulder

for it to be broken for it to be a head and shoulders position. The pattern can occur on a slope. The price is supposed to reach as far below the neckline as the top of the head is from the neckline.

The position can also occur as a bullish pattern if it appears as an opposite mirror reflection. In that case, the price would break up through the neckline. In many ways, you can think of the neckline as a support and trade the pattern like a trendline break as mentioned earlier.

Tops and bottoms strategies

A bottom is the opposite of, wait for it, a ... top (Diagram 5.11). The top occurs where the price rises to a resistance level, falls back, rises and again falls back. The volume on the rise to the second peak should be lower than the volume on the rise to the first peak.

This is because buyers are getting weaker at pushing the price up. The valley to peak should be at least 15 percent to represent a proper top. As buyers lose numbers and heart, the sellers push the price down and a reversal occurs.

Triangle strategies

Diagram 5.12 shows a triangle. For a price reversal on the upside the horizontal line appears above the ascending diagonal line. We

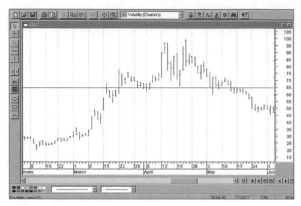

DIAGRAM 5.11 ■ You're the tops

DIAGRAM 5.12 ■ A triangle

are then looking for a breakout through the horizontal line. To trade the pattern you can treat it very much like a breakout pattern from a resistance level.

The last example is an ascending triangle; the descending triangle is an exact mirror reflection and that would represent a price breakout to the downside. In the ascending triangle pattern, buyers are willing to pay increasingly higher prices but at the resistance level their willingness subsides and sellers come in.

Near the pinnacle of the triangle, the buyers overcome the sellers and a breakout occurs.

Volume should be decreasing to the apex and then increase on breakout as the marauding purchasing invaders breach the sellers' line of defence. The triangle pattern occurs quite frequently and the price target is as far above the horizontal as the mouth of the triangle is wide! Why that should be the price target is a bit of a mystery.

Saucer strategies

The pattern for this is shown in Diagram 5.13. It represents a gradual change in opinion about a stock. Although saucers are rare, if you can spot them as the price is rising they can be an additional confirmatory indicator of a trend change. There are no price targets for this pattern, so exit needs to be determined more by rising stop losses or by the other technical methods we discuss in the following sections.

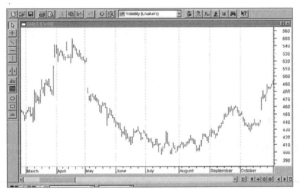

DIAGRAM 5.13 ■ A flying pattern – the saucer

Continuation patterns

These patterns confirm that the current direction of price movement will continue. They can represent a pause in price and so can be used as a good point to step on before the escalator starts moving up again.

Rectangles: not a square strategy

The rectangle is simply where the price action moves sideways between a support and resistance level after a rise (see Diagram 5.14). It can be thought of as a resting place where buying and selling troops stop for a moment to reconsider price levels; some start to profit, while other latecomers get on board.

A strategy for this is to trade it in the same way you would any other breakout through a resistance (forgotten? – we *have* discussed it already). Once the breakout occurs prices should continue onwards and upwards. Unlike just a plain breakout through a resistance level, the fact that there has been a rectangle formation first and a price rise before it adds to the likelihood of a breakout from the resistance.

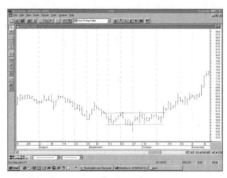

DIAGRAM 5.14 ■ Rectangle

Flag strategy: flying the flag for more of the same

A flag can appear in an uptrend or downtrend. See Diagram 5.15 for an example. The flag looks like a rectangle rotated diagonally upward and is preceded by a downtrend. The flag is where instead of a sideways move after a downturn, buyers for a while outgun sellers and cause prices to rise as they believe prices have oversold, but the sellers soon return as prices rise. The flag is important only after the bottom of the flag is pierced – so wait for that. Then you know the market will fall further and you see a flag. If it is not pierced, you simply have a reversal.

DIAGRAM 5.15 ■ The price continues to flag

Pennant strategy

The pennant is like other continuation patterns in that it forms as
a breathing space in the battle between buyers and sellers. In
Diagram 5.16 you can see a clear example.

DIAGRAM 5.16 ■ A pennant

The pennant in the example shows a rising trend followed by a price move where two boundary lines converge, representing the battle between buyers and sellers. Volume should decrease to the apex and increase on the breakout through the upper boundary.

You can treat the breakout through the upper boundary in the same way for trading as we said before when discussing trading breakouts generally. The pennant just makes a breakout more likely to result in a continuation than a simple breakout without a pennant.

Momentum-based strategies

Momentum is a generic term I am using here to discuss four similar indicators: stochastic, momentum, MACD (see later) and RSI (an indicator is basically a plotted line based on a mathematical formula and the stock price).

The reasoning behind all momentum indicators is that a security price moving in a particular direction tends to slow before reversing direction. Therefore, if we can pinpoint where it has started slowing, we can be ready for the reversal and plan our strategies accordingly. Think of prices as a ball thrown in the air: before the ball reverses it tends to slow down. Indicators try to depict that in a graphical format.

> * A security price moving in a particular direction tends to slow before reversing direction

Time frames

All the indicators discussed so far are based on mathematical operations undertaken on price. You do not need to worry about what the specifics are, but, for those interested, stay with me.

These formulae have one or two, sometimes three, variables that affect how the indicators are displayed and the time frame for which they will give the best signals. Most software and sites already incorporate as default settings the most popular values for the variables and so, again, you do not need to worry about that. You can just experiment with different variable values to see what produces the best results. So, onwards now to the issue of how to interpret these indicators so that you can base some strategies around them.

You would rarely base a buy or sell decision on just one of the following indicators. We are always looking for as much evidence as possible about a price move in a particular direction and towards the end we shall see how a professional technical analyst would do it.

Overbought/oversold strategies

All the momentum indicators can be used to indicate how overbought or oversold a security is. For illustration let us stick to oversold, which is the opposite of overbought. We say a security is oversold when selling has forced the price down so much that it should bounce back. So how do the momentum indicators measure this?

Looking at Diagram 5.17, which plots the momentum indicator, we would say that the security is oversold when the momentum indicator is near its extreme lows relative to its other lows. Now, you can get more precise and say that the security is oversold if the momentum is below a specific figure.

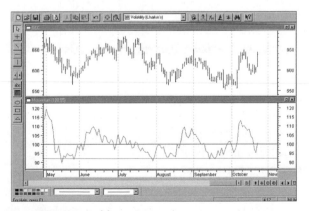

DIAGRAM 5.17 ■ Momentum

Trading strategy

One way to trade oversold signals is to buy the security when the momentum indicator moves up from being oversold. This is way too simple a strategy to be consistently profitable. So why am I telling you and why is it too simple?

Even though it is too simple a strategy in itself, it is a useful piece of evidence to add to the whole melting pot of which way we think prices may go. It is too simple because momentum indicators often go oversold, go up a little out of oversold territory and then become oversold again. Also, we must remember, price has to be our ultimate indicator and we must wait for the price to move up as well, because the momentum indicator could continue up, but prices continue down.

One way to use this evidence in conjunction with any other evidence of an impending price move may be if the momentum is oversold and just starts moving up and the price is in a rectangle formation and just starts a breakout. You would have more confidence in the move because you have two independent strategies confirming that the move is less likely to be a false move (see Diagram 5.18).

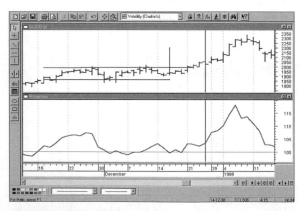

DIAGRAM 5.18 ■ Trading strategy

Positive divergence

Improving on oversold signals is positive divergence. Check out Diagram 5.19. A positive divergence occurs when the momentum indicator (whether the momentum, stochastic, MACD or RSI) makes a higher low, but the price does not make a corresponding higher low; instead it makes a lower low.

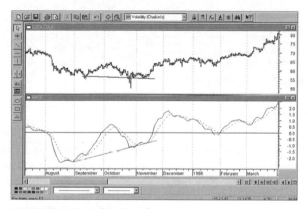

DIAGRAM 5.19 ■ Positive divergence

Trading strategy

One popular strategy is to buy as the momentum and the price rise after the price makes its higher low. This is not foolproof but is more reliable and more favoured by technical analysts than simply oversold signals.

Negative divergence

Diagram 5.20 illustrates a negative divergence. The momentum indicator makes lower highs while the price does not or even makes higher highs. As the momentum indicator then starts to fall from its high (which should be in overbought territory) so should the price. Again this is a stronger signal of an impending price fall than just a straightforward oversold signal.

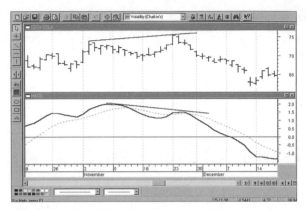

DIAGRAM 5.20 ■ Negative divergence

Trading strategy

Go short or exit a long position as the price and momentum start to dip. To avoid a bad signal, you could incorporate a rule like: 'The momentum has to fall from an oversold position and the price has to break the previous day's low before you exit or go short.'

Reverse divergence

The reverse divergence is a variation on the theme just examined. It occurs when the price makes lower highs but the momentum makes higher highs deeper into oversold territory. Diagram 5.21 shows an example. The price should fall with the momentum indicator now.

Trading strategy

You can decide to exit or go short as the momentum and price both move downwards from the momentum's oversold position.

Momentum trendlines

Trendlines on momentum indicators as in Diagram 5.22 can sometimes give clues to possible price movement where no trendline can be drawn on the price chart.

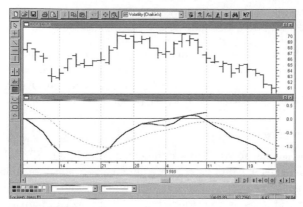

DIAGRAM 5.21 ■ Reverse divergence

DIAGRAM 5.22 ■ Mo' better trendlines

Trading strategy

The trendline on the momentum can be used in the same way as in normal price indicators. So, for instance, a resistance level on the momentum indicator may give a good indication that an imminent price reversal is about to occur. The same cautions with corroborating indicators and price confirmation apply as before, i.e. make sure you have another indicator or chart pattern confirming the bearishness and wait until prices fall.

Stochastics

While the stochastic is a momentum-based indicator and the interpretations and strategies explained thus far can be applied to it, there are also some specifics to it because of its design. Diagram 5.23 shows a stochastic and price chart.

%K crosses %D

With the stochastic you can see there is a solid line (%K) and a dotted line (%D). Don't worry about the mathematical formulae that generate them. Stochastic followers will consider a buy signal when the %K crosses up through the %D in an oversold territory as in Diagram 5.23. A sell signal is when the %K crosses down through the %D and both are in overbought territory. When combined with the other pattern, such positive divergences can be quite a powerful indicator.

False divergence

This pattern occurs when the %K approaches the %D and looks like it is going to cross it and be a buy signal, but instead it just teases us by kissing it and rebounding off it. This can be a strong signal of a price continuing to fall. Diagram 5.24 shows an example of this. It can also occur as a bullish pattern as in Diagram 5.25.

Stochastic compared to the RSI and momentum indicators

I tend to find the stochastic less prone to false signals which see me enter, only to have the price then not do as expected. The stochastic is not a volatile indicator and gives smoother, easier-to-read lines. I like it.

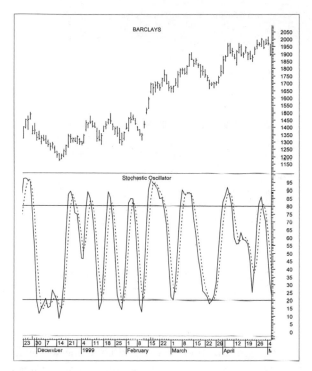

DIAGRAM 5.23 ■ Stochastics

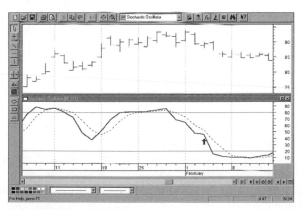

DIAGRAM 5.24 ■ Teaser

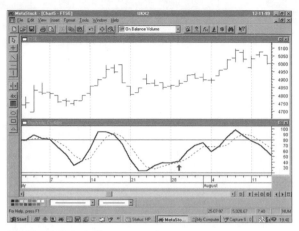

DIAGRAM 5.25 ■ Teaser

The weaknesses in stochastics, momentum and RSI

If we understand the weaknesses of certain indicators we can, hopefully, avoid traps of poor trades and compensate for those weaknesses by adding new indicators which do not suffer the same weaknesses. The stochastic, momentum and RSI can all waver in the oversold or overbought regions for prolonged periods of time when a trend is continuing onwards in the same direction. So you could get a false signal to sell prematurely during an uptrend as the oversold indicator suggests a sell signal. Diagram 5.26 illustrates this problem.

The question then arises of how we can solve the problem. One way is not to act on a signal until the price confirms it. So, for instance, you would not act on a sell signal from the momentum indicator unless the price closes lower than the previous day's low and then opens the next day and moves lower. Another way to avoid the premature signal is to observe both the momentum indicator and the MACD. So let us turn now to the MACD. (Not a bad link, eh?)

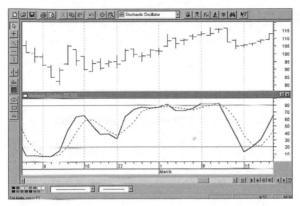

DIAGRAM 5.26 ■ New indicators

MACD (pronounced Mac-D like the famous chain of burger joints)

Not named after a Scotsman, but standing for the moving average convergence divergence, the MACD by its mathematical construction does not tend to suffer from the problems of the other momentum indicators. Diagram 5.27 illustrates this.

The dotted line is the moving average of the MACD and is called the signal line. A crossing of the solid line from above in the overbought region can be interpreted as a sell signal and a move up of the dotted line through the solid line when in the oversold region is a buy signal.

Trading strategy

The MACD tends to give fewer buy or sell signals than the other momentum indicators. I tend to use it to avoid the problems with the momentum indicators giving premature signals. So for instance in Diagram 5.28 we see the momentum indicator suggest a buy signal but the MACD is dropping so sharply that it overrides the momentum signal.

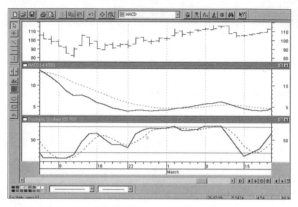

DIAGRAM 5.27 ■ MACD

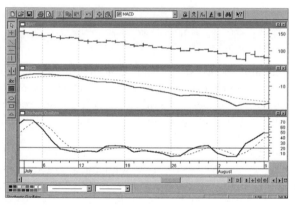

DIAGRAM 5.28 ■ Strategy

Why not use MACD all the time? Well, I think it works best when combined with the momentum indicators because the MACD is a little bit slow and tends to give buy signals a bit too late. So a better strategy is to buy based on the momentum indicators as long as the MACD is not falling sharply and possibly has even just started moving sideways. See Diagram 5.29 for an illustration.

Hence we can use the stochastic and the MACD together.

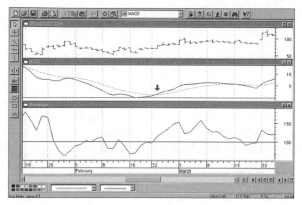

DIAGRAM 5.29 ■ MACD in combination

The MACD is better used as a longer term indicator. It reveals more about the market background and the broader trend. Once we are convinced the trend is upward as indicated by the MACD and by looking at the price diagram we can turn to the stochastic to give us some indication of the shorter term price move.

Great buying opportunities stem from when a stock is oversold in the short term, as indicated by the stochastic, but in a longer term uptrend, as indicated by the MACD (see Diagram 5.30).

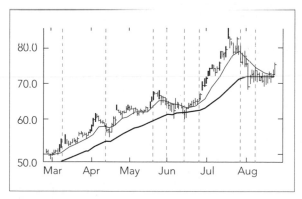

DIAGRAM 5.30 ■ Great buying opportunities

Summary

So, to summarize, it is a good time to buy into a security if we identify an uptrend and then buy on weakness on the uptrend – for instance as the momentum indicators fall to an oversold position on the uptrend. As the uptrend resumes, the stock price will move up and you will have got in at a relatively cheap price.

In Diagram 5.31 (look at where I have inserted the horizontal line) the MACD is trending upward and so is the stock, suggesting medium-term strong buy or hold opportunity. However, in the short term it is oversold. The price has dipped. This is where the stochastic comes in. It is telling us that the short-term situation is oversold and we may want to buy in at that relatively cheap level.

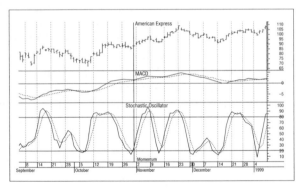

DIAGRAM 5.31 ■ How to exploit the stochastic

6

The anatomy of a price rise and strategy rules

Online trader problems

- What is it about price moves and indicators that makes making profits so difficult?
- If I know this what can I do to avoid problems?

In this chapter

Making trading rules by which to enter, let alone exit, the market, can sometimes feel like trying to solve the Rubik Cube: you get one bit right (for instance, the number of losing trades is low) only to find that another bit is not quite right (the profits from your remaining trades drop). In this chapter we examine the nature of a price move and what you should know before designing your own rules or using someone else's.

Price moves

If you are looking to go long the market, then, ideally, you want an indicator that will get you in as close to the bottom of the rise as possible. The problem with many indicators is that they are either too early (so that the market keeps dropping after you enter, only for you to find that it knocks out your stop loss, or to find you should have entered later to make more money) or too late (in which case you often find you make very little profit because the bulk of the move has gone) or, worse, the signal is so late the trend has reversed (see Table 6.1).

Don't worry, there will be pictures to go with the words (see Diagrams 6.1–6.7).

Consider the nature of the start of an upward price move (see Diagram 6.3).

TABLE 6.1 ■ Price moves and indicators

	Indicator or entry rule triggered too early		Indicator or entry rule triggered too late	
Price action	Price continues dropping after entry, then rises	Price continues dropping after entry then drops some more	Price has only a little further to rise	Price turns around and now starts to fall back
Consequence	Little profit, You miss out on some profit	You make a loss	Little profit	You make a loss

The price stops dipping and rises a little. At point **x** some indicator, let us say the momentum indicator, will signal a buy. It could be any indicator, but for this illustration we are assuming that a signal is generated at that point. When you develop your own rules you will find that some of your tests result in a signal at that early point. At point **y**, another indicator, let us say the stochastic, will generate a signal.

Now, as things stand one of three things could happen. From point **y**, the price could dip and move higher, it could dip and dip lower or not dip and just keep rising. As matters stand, all things being equal, we do not know *what* will happen when we are at point **y**. Of course, looking at other indicators and factors we may conclude that one event is more *probable* than another, but we never *know*. That is what makes trading difficult. It is all probabilities.

If the price dipped and then dipped even lower and you entered at **x** on the indications of the momentum indicator then by the time you got out you would not have suffered as big a loss compared to getting in at point **y**. The other benefit of getting in at point **x** is that if the price actually dips and rises, then you would make a bigger profit than if you got in at **y** and also would probably not ever go into negative territory.

> ✳ **That is what makes trading difficult. It is all probabilities**

So, you prefer indicators that give a buy signal at **x** over those that give it slightly later at **y**? But that seems too obvious. Well, the problem with indicators that give buy signals at **x** is that they are triggered by a small price rise that can occur so often in everyday declines, i.e. it generates many false signals. The small price rise that triggers the buy signal at **x** does not trigger the signal at **y**. So **y** avoids lots of small losses. We now have a trade-off to face.

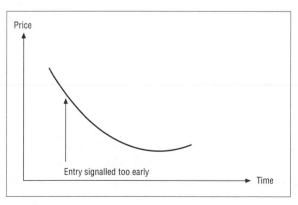

DIAGRAM 6.1 ■ Indicator too early

The early indicator gives us more profit compared to the later one if the price continues upward and less of a loss if the price dips after triggering the later indicator. But all this comes at the expense of having more losing trades that are avoided by the later indicator.

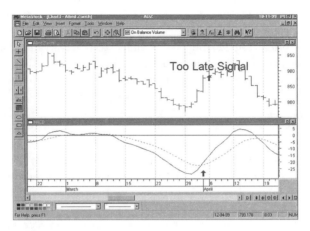

DIAGRAM 6.2 ■ Indicator too late

DIAGRAM 6.3 ■ Start of an upward price move

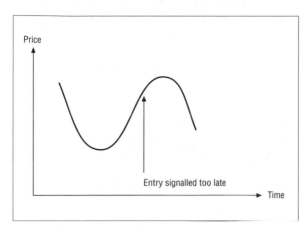

DIAGRAM 6.4 ■ Price dips

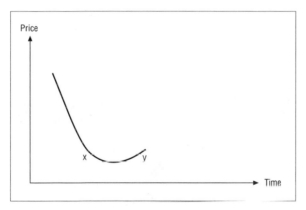

DIAGRAM 6.5 ■ Price moves higher

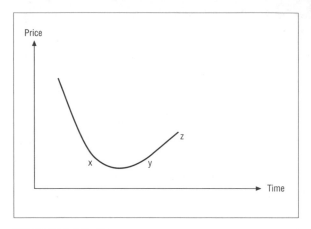

DIAGRAM 6.6 ■ Price goes up

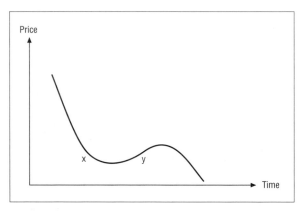

DIAGRAM 6.7 ■ Price dips lower

What should you do?

The prime concern in any system is what makes more money, the system triggered at **x** or at **y** and that is the determinant. I have often found that the indicator giving the buy signal at **y** is the one that is more profitable because it avoids all the false losing signals of the signal at **x**. So that is settled, then, is it?

The problem is that as soon as you get the signal at **y** you can do one of two things the next morning:

1 You could buy on the open. This is not recommended because if you had waited and saw the price fall, you could have saved yourself from a bad trade or entered later at a better price.

2 You could wait to see if the price rises and then buy. This is what I prefer to do. But if only life were that easy. What do you do if the price does indeed fall from the open, but at the close your indicator still says buy?

Well, you go with what the price is doing, not what the indicator is saying. If the indicator says buy and the next morning the price falls, you should not buy.

When do you get in?

I would wait for the price to break the preceding day's high or break the level it reached when the buy signal was first given. (I know all this seems convoluted, but you will encounter these questions and wonder what on earth to do, so persevere.) This way, if the price keeps falling, you are OK because you never got in. But, on the downside, all this waiting means you could enter at such a late stage that the whole move has expired (see Diagram 6.4 again).

> *I would wait for the price to break the preceding day's high or break the level it reeached when the buy signal was first given*

It is this that may well make you think the market is out to get you and you feel it has led you up the garden path like some teasing amorous lover, only to have the door slammed in your face before you could get . . . some. Another analogy is the market as a bucking bronco trying to throw you off. Fear not, she teases everyone, do not become paranoid; that is the way of the markets.

Now look at Diagram 6.8.

Do you get in at **x**, **y** or **z**? I prefer the indicator that gives the signal at **y** and if the price dips immediately after the signal is generated, I try to get in as soon as possible on an uptick (i.e. slight price rise) but not as late as **z**. This way I miss the losses incurred by getting in too early at **x** and too late at **z**.

DIAGRAM 6.8 ■ When did you get in?

Summary

In system and trading rule design you will definitely come across the problem in diagram 40, so it is good to know it exists; others have had to deal with it. It involves trade-offs, but ultimately the guiding decision is 'what makes the most money in the long term?' Remember, you may not always encounter this problem, the price may just go up and up and up and not dip until well after you have got buy signals from your system. But on the whole, price rise and dip and indicators come in three flavours; early, intermediate, late. I have tried to convey what I believe generally to be the optimal strategy.

7

Fundamentals

The real measure of your wealth is how much you'd be worth if you lost all your money.

Anon

In this chapter

Let's have a look at a whole host of popular methods for trading ideas. We will want to examine the company's balance sheet for a start and get a feel for how the company is doing.

- Trading around an earnings announcement is also a popular way of trading for some people and we'll see how that is done and how to use specific sites to do it.

- Similarly, when upgrades or downgrades are issued on a stock, we want to know where we can find these announcements and how we can use them for our trading to find lower risk, higher return trades.

- Some traders like to see if the company's inside officers, such as directors, are trading its stock – we need to examine how that works and how to use it.

And potential stock-split candidates and post-split stocks can also be an interesting way of trading – again, we'll look at which the sites are, exactly what the thinking is behind this trading method and how we can join in.

Objectives

■ Broadly understand how to read fundamental information about a stock.

■ Get an idea about how to find upgrades and earnings information, how to find out the level of insider trading and if there are stock splits and how to use that information as a basis of gaining stock ideas.

Growth rates

Table 7.1 shows growth rates as they appear on Standard & Poor's 500 index.

TABLE 7.1 ■ Growth rates (%)

Company	Industry	Sector	S&P 500
Sales (MRQ) vs qtr 1 year ago	9.08*	7.92	19.47
Sales (TTM) vs TTM 1 year ago	8.88*	8.30	26.89
Sales – 5-year growth rate	9.85	13.15	22.43
EPS (MRQ) vs qtr 1 year ago	–13.79*	5.39	25.44
EPS (TTM) vs TTM 1 year ago	–3.92*	3.84	23.49
EPS – 5-year growth rate	12.66	14.13	21.84
Capital spending – 5-year growth rate	14.20	15.81	28.30

Sales growth

A company can perform well over the short term with rising earnings even if sales are dropping. This can occur if profits (earnings) are being increased due to cost cutting. However, there will come a time when costs cannot be lowered any further and decreasing sales growth feeds back into lower earnings. For that reason examining sales growth is important.

Earnings per share growth

EPS growth is a key factor feeding into company growth.

The year-to-year comparison for the most recent quarter (MRQ) represents the most up-to-date growth information available to the financial community and is always an important determinant of near-term stock price performance. Assume that strong MRQ growth rates will be accompanied by strong stock price performance and vice versa. If that is not the case then examine the news reports to find out why.

> *Assume that strong MRQ growth rates will be accompanied by strong stock price performance*

Market Guide explains that when examining company-to-industry capital spending comparisons, remember that it is normal for a business to spend at least some money for capital projects year in, year out. But at times capital spending can mushroom to especially high levels as a major project ramps up and then slide to a lesser pace as the newly completed project allows the company to trim down to basic 'maintenance' levels.

> *If you see that a company's capital spending growth was significantly higher than that of its industry, that could suggest that the company's needs should moderate, relative to its peers, in the next few years*

If you see that a company's capital spending growth was significantly higher than that of its industry, that could suggest that the company's needs should moderate, relative to its peers, in the next few years. That would give the company more flexibility regarding the use of its cash flow (dividends, share buy-backs, acquisitions, etc.). If you see that growth in spending trailed the industry average, that might suggest pent-up capital needs (and increased spending) in the years ahead.

Finally, compare the five-year growth rates for capital spending and sales. This can be important since there's usually a relationship between the value of a company's assets and the amount of sales that those assets can generate. A rate of sales growth that exceeds the rate of capital spending growth might indicate that a company is finding new ways to generate more revenues from existing plant. But it could also mean that capacity is getting tight and that capital spending increases are just around the corner.

Valuation ratios

These are essential. They give me an idea of whether I am picking up a bargain, a fairly priced stock or an expensive one. For me the key is price trend, so valuations do not veto a stock selection but if all other things were equal, I would want a lower valued stock.

Alternatively some investors focus purely on valuations and this can be a useful gauge of a company's potential.

Price to earnings

The p/e ratio shows you the multiple you're paying for each dollar of earnings of the company. One would normally prefer a company with a lower p/e to one with higher p/e. However, note

A stock is attractive if its p/e ratio is lower than its long-term compound growth rate in EPS

that there can be little wrong with paying a higher p/e multiple for a rapidly growing company because you expect its future earnings rate to be higher.

A good rule of thumb is that a stock is attractive if its p/e ratio is lower than its long-term compound growth rate in EPS.

Conversely, a company with a low p/e ratio is not necessarily a good thing. It may be because its outlook is more uncertain due to factors such as competition, a lawsuit or a cyclical downturn. I tend to look for p/e lower than the industry average.

As well as p/e, examining other similar ratios is always very useful (and definitely impresses the opposite sex in bars – go ahead and try it); these are price to sales (which is especially useful for early-stage growth companies that might not have reached profitability), price to book value and price to cash flow. Each provides a slightly different perspective and I look on them as an artist not as a scientist; in other words, I try to get a broad, general feel for the figures rather than requiring them to be very exact.

Beta

Beta measures stock price volatility relative to the overall stock market. So, for instance, if we use the S&P 500 as a proxy for the market as a whole and we automatically define its beta as being 1.00, then a higher beta indicates that a stock is more volatile while a lower beta indicates stability. For example, a stock with a beta of 0.90 would, on average, be expected to rise or fall only 90 percent as much as the market. So if the market dropped 10 percent, such a stock might rise or fall 9 percent.

Price to sales

Price to sales is generally used to evaluate companies that don't have earnings and that don't pay dividends – in recent times that has often meant internet companies. For these companies, you may consider that high multiples of sales and high growth rates suggest optimistic future earnings expectations on the part of investors. Where earnings have wild swings in any particular year, for instance due to one-off items, price to sales can be a good indicator of the underlying health of the company.

Price to book

Price to book is a theoretical comparison of the value of the company's stock to the value of the assets it owns (free and clear of debt). This is probably of less importance in practice than it is in theory. The idea behind it is that book value is a proxy for the proceeds that would be realized if the company were to be liquidated by selling all its assets and paying off all its debt.

In reality, though, assets are valued on the books at the actual prices the company paid to acquire them, minus cumulative depreciation/amortization charges. The idea behind these costs is gradually to reduce the value of the assets to zero over a period of use in which they approach obsolescence. However, this is based on specific accounting formulae that may not resemble 'real-world' time to obsolescence.

And remember that for a services company the 'book value' does not produce the revenue. So all in all, I tend to ignore this.

Cash flow and net income

Net income gives us some idea of 'how much money the company is generating' which in turn may give us an idea of the health and wealth of the company. To calculate net income, we subtract all expenses from revenues. Unfortunately, things are never quite that simple.

For instance, a manufacturing firm spends $10 million to build a factory that will help it create products for a period of ten years. We would recognize factory construction expenses of $10 million in year one and zero in each of years two to ten. This would suggest one unusually poor year for profits, followed by nine very good ones.

The preferred practice is to match revenues as closely as possible to the expenses incurred to generate those revenues. In

> *The preferred practice is to match revenues as closely as possible to the expenses incurred to generate those revenues

our example, we assume that the $10 million factory generates ten years' worth of revenues so we apportion one-tenth of the $10 million outlay in each of those ten years. This one-tenth charge is known as depreciation (amortization is a similar annual charge for a different sort of one-off expenditure that is matched against more than one year's worth of sales).

So, how should an investor assess all of this? Well, keep on reading.

As well as net income we would want to look at cash flow as an indicator of corporate health and strength.

If you want to know how much the company can afford to pay in dividends or use for other investments, you would look to the cash flow, which is calculated by adding non-cash depreciation and amortization charges back to net income.

- But cash flow alone doesn't give us the full story.

- Free cash flow looks at the cash the company's operations actually generated in a given year and subtracts important 'non-operating' cash outlays, capital spending and dividend payments.

- Accordingly, free cash flow is the purest measure of a company's capacity to generate cash.

- Cash flow is a less pure number, but also less susceptible to wide year-to-year swings as capital programmes periodically build up and wind down.

- Clearly, we are looking to compare price to cash flow and price to free cash flow relative to other companies in the same industry and also to see how cash flow and free cash flow change year on year for the company in order to gauge a measure of its growth and valuation.

- We want price to cash flow ratios to be low relative to other companies in the same industry and we want cash flow to be rising year on year.

Let's take a closer look at cash flows (yes, it may feel tedious – but, believe me, it's good for you) (see Table 7.2).

The *statement of cash flow* from Market Guide shown in Table 7.2 is divided into three sections:

The *operating* section tells you how the company's basic business performed.

The *investing* section will highlight capital expenditures, purchase of investment securities and acquisitions. This is how

TABLE 7.2 ■ Selected statement of cash flow (CF) items (indirect method)

	Annual			Year to date	
	12 months ending 31/12/95	12 months ending 31/12/96	12 months ending 31/12/97	9 months ending 30/09/97	9 months ending 30/09/98
Net income	1 427 300	1 572 600	1 642 500	1 231 600	1 201 600
Depreciation and amortization	709 000	742 900	793 800	557 000	648 300
Non-cash items	–4 200	32 900	–110 700	0	0
Other operating CF	164 100	112 600	116 700	–68 400	147 500
Total operating CF	2 296 200	2 461 000	2 442 300	1 720 200	1 997 400
Capital expenditures	–2 063 700	–2 375 300	–2 111 200	–1 444 000	–1 350 100
Other investing CF	–45 300	–195 000	–106 000	–102 200	–50 100
Total investing CF	–2 109 000	–2 570 300	–2 217 200	–1 546 200	–1 400 200
Dividends paid	–226 500	–232 000	–247 700	–186 300	–179 500
Sale (purchases) of stock	–314 500	–599 900	–1 113 100	–568 400	–1 049 100
Net borrowings	445 100	779 300	1 001 500	415 000	390 100
Other financing CF	63 600	157 000	145 700	146 000	204 200
Total financing CF	–32 300	104 400	–213 600	–193 700	–634 300
Exchange rate effect	0	0	0	0	0
Net change in cash	154 900	–4 900	11 500	–19 700	–37 100

Note: Units in thousands of US dollars

the company has invested its money for the future.

The *financing* section shows if the company borrowed money or if the company issued or repurchased shares. The *net change in cash* is equal to the net effects of what the company generates in operations, spends to invest for the future, how it finances itself and the impact of foreign currency adjustments.

You want to see a company in which *net income plus depreciation are greater than capital expenditures plus dividend payments*. This is the definition of *free cash flow*. If a company has free cash flow, then it can finance its growth and finance its dividend payments from internal sources. If a company doesn't have a positive free cash flow, it may have to sell equity (which will dilute your holdings), borrow money, sell assets or use its working capital more efficiently.

> ✳ If a company has free cash flow, then it can finance its growth and finance its dividend payments from internal sources

The cash flow statement provides insight into which of these sources funded the company's activities in the period(s) in question.

Some of the items to look for in the statement of cash flows include:

- positive and growing cash from operations
- large and growing capital expenditures meaning that the company is investing in its future
- repurchase of stock represented by a negative number (as it is a use of cash) is generally positive; sales of stock (positive values) are generally negative unless explained by rapid growth which often requires additional equity capital
- a negative number for net borrowings indicating a repayment of debt is generally positive. A profitable company with low financial leverage taking on some new debt may also be positive. A highly leveraged company taking on more debt can be dangerous.

Share-related items

For me, market capitalization just provides an idea of how big the company is that I am investing in: it is not a trade breaker. It is the stock price multiplied by the number of shares outstanding. This is the benchmark on which a company is classified as one of the following:

- large cap (capitalization greater than $5 billion)
- mid-cap (capitalization between $1 billion and $5 billion)
- small cap (capitalization between $300 million and $1 billion)
- micro cap (capitalization below $300 million).

Larger companies tend to be safer to invest in than small companies, although several studies indicate that while riskier, the smaller companies as a group tend to outperform larger companies over long periods of time. I tend to focus more on smaller and some micro cap companies, sprinkled with a few safer large caps like Telecom Italia, Cisco, Sun, Oracle, TelMex, Apple and Nokia.

The shares outstanding is the number of shares issued by the company less any shares the company has bought back. The float indicates the number of shares held by everybody other than officers, directors and 5 percent or more owners. If there is little float, there's generally very little trading volume and anybody wishing to buy or sell the stock may impact the price significantly.

Dividend information

The annual dividend is the total amount of dividends you could expect to receive if you held the stock for a year and there were no change in the company's dividend payment. It is based on the current quarterly dividend payment rate projected forward for four quarters. Since I look for growth companies I prefer it if the company reinvests its dividend rather than paying it to shareholders.

There was a time when a company not paying a dividend could expect to have its share price punished by virtue of the fact that many conservative funds looking for income rather than capital growth from their stocks would steer clear of such companies. Higher yields on stocks can suggest Wall Street expectations of sluggish growth. The dividend yield is:

- The indicated annual dividend rate expressed as a percentage of the price of the stock and could be compared to the coupon yield on a bond.

- It allows you to see how much income you can expect per $ or £ investment from this stock, so allowing you to compare it with other stocks you may be looking at.

- Some prefer high yield, others low.

- If you are looking for high-growth companies as a general rule, all other things being equal, you will prefer low-yield companies.

The *payout ratio* tells you what percentage of the company's earnings have been given to shareholders as cash dividends over the past 12 months. I look for stocks with a low payout ratio, which indicates that the company has chosen to reinvest most of the profits back into the business.

There are a few sectors whose stocks are regarded as income vehicles – utility and real estate in particular. Investors in these sectors focus more on yields than those in other sectors.

Management effectiveness

The management effectiveness is about return on capital. If you invest in government bonds, you would know you are going to get a certain return: the 'risk-free rate of return'. Since investments in businesses are riskier you would be expecting a better return than the risk-free one.

Return on equity

The shareholders of a company can be thought of as having given a company capital – or equity. The return on equity (ROE) is a measure of how effectively the company has managed this equity. Equity represents that portion of the company's assets that would be distributed to shareholders if the company were liquidated and all assets sold at values reflected on the company's balance sheet, so it is what the company itself and therefore the shareholders own and does not include, for instance, money loaned from a bank.

Return on investment

Since return on investment (ROI) relates only to capital provided by shareholders, it is a limited measure of management effectiveness since we also want to know how the company is performing with the other sources of money at its disposal. Return on investment shows how effective management is in utilizing money provided by the company's owners (equity) and long-term creditors.

Return on assets

As well as shareholder capital and long-term money granted to the company there are also shorter term loans of capital and so return on assets (ROA) is a broader measure than the preceding two of how a company is handling funds provided to it. For example, an internet company may borrow money to purchase some Sun Microsystems routers for its website. The lender may be providing short-term (i.e. less than one year) credit. Return on assets measures management's effectiveness in using everything at its disposal (equity, long-term credit and temporary capital) to produce profits.

Profitability

Profitability ratios relate to how much of the revenue the company receives is being turned into profit.

Gross margin shows you what percentage of each revenue dollar is left after deducting direct costs of producing the goods or services which in turn bring in the revenue. For a services company, the most common direct costs would be employees' salaries.

The money left at this stage is called gross profit. Gross margin expresses the relationship between gross profit and revenues in percentage terms. For example, a gross margin of 10 percent means that ten cents out of every revenue dollar are left after deducting direct costs.

Operating profit and *operating margin* follow the progress of each revenue dollar to another important level. From gross profit we now subtract indirect costs, often referred to as overheads. Examples of overheads would be the costs associated with headquarters operations: costs that are essential to the business, but not directly connected to any single individual product manufactured and sold by the company.

Finally, *net profit* and the *net margin* show you how much of each revenue dollar is left after all costs, of any kind, are subtracted, such as interest on corporate debt and income taxes. High margins are better than low margins and this applies equally when comparing companies in the same industry.

Tax rates

Profitability is also affected by tax rates. A company may have an unusually low tax rate because of losses carried forward or other temporary issues. These will vanish in the future and could sharply affect the profitability of the company. Consequently, it is a good thing to see if the company has an unusually low tax rate.

Recommendations

Ultimately, everything you do when you analyze a stock boils down to what you'll find in this report: specific investment decisions. The recommendations table (Table 7.3) tells you exactly what professional securities analysts who cover the company have decided to do regarding its stock.

TABLE 7.3 ■ Analyst recommendations and revisions

	As of 22/04/1999	As of 4 weeks ago	As of 8 weeks ago	As of 12 weeks ago
1 Strong buy	1.6	1.5	NA	NA
2 Buy	1.8	1.7	NA	NA
3 Hold	1.7	1.7	NA	NA
4 Underperform	1.0	1.0	NA	NA
5 Sell	1.0	1.0	NA	NA
Mean rating	2.0	2.1	NA	NA

Table 7.3 contains five possible investment recommendations: strong buy, buy, hold, underperform and sell. They are based on the five recommendation categories used by most investment advisory organizations. The terminology may vary from one firm to another (for example, some might label the third recommendation 'neutral' instead of 'hold'). But whatever set of labels you see, you can *assume that the investment advisors are ranking stocks in a five-step, best-to-worst sequence.*

Critics of Wall Street research point out that brokerage firm analysts are quick to recommend purchases of stock, but almost never advise customers to sell. You can evaluate this by examining Market Guide recommendation tables for a large number of stocks.

If you do that, you are very likely to find that 'underperform' and 'sell' recommendations are extremely rare; 'neutral' ratings aren't quite so scarce, but they do appear far less frequently than do 'strong buy' and 'buy' recommendations. Fortunately for you, I/B/E/S compiles, and Market Guide presents, additional information that enables you to derive worthwhile real-world Wall Street recommendations despite the fact that analyst ratings tend to cluster towards the top of the scale.

The last row of the table presents the mean rating. This is a weighted average of all the individual ratings. The best possible score would be 1.0 (to achieve that, every analyst would have to rate the stock a 'strong buy') and the worst possible score would be 5.0. Realistically, given the aforementioned top-of-the-rating-scale bias, you should expect most mean ratings to fall in the 1.00–3.00 range. But within that context, you still can, and should, *compare a stock's mean rating to those of others you are considering and favour those with better (i.e. lower number) scores.*

Also, *look at the columns showing the recommendations four, eight and 12 weeks ago.*

■ If you are a momentum investor, you will want to favour stocks for which there are a gradually increasing number of top recommendations or improving mean rating scores.

■ Those who prefer out-of-favour stocks may take a different approach. Such investors would prefer stocks for which the mean rating has been deteriorating.

A mean rating that is stable (or modestly better) from the four-week-ago period to the present after having deteriorated from the 12- to eight- to four-week-ago intervals might be especially interesting. This trend could be signalling the early stages of a turnaround. A gradual increase in the number of recommendations over the past 12 weeks would indicate that Wall Street is turning its eye toward a company that had previously been ignored or undiscovered.

Performance

Excellent sites like Market Guide provide data allowing you to compare price performance of stocks relative to major indices and the industry they are in. You can also get a feel for this from sites with graphing facilities. These are mainly viewed in two ways by most people.

Value investors may look for underperformers on the basis that these stocks will eventually 'catch up' with the rest of the index, even if in the short term they will underperform and drag down a whole portfolio. Growth investors may well look for those that lead the market in terms of performance.

For instance, the Market Guide price performance table (Table 7.4) shows you the stock's percentage price movements over each of five measurement periods: four weeks, 13 weeks, 26 weeks, 52 weeks and year to date (YTD). Large percentage changes, as shown in the second (actual %) column, will obviously catch your eye. But the other three columns are the ones that can add important depth to your understanding of the stock's recent performance.

TABLE 7.4 ■ Price performance

Period	Actual (%)	S&P 500 (%)	Rank in industry	Industry rank
4-week	5.2	–1.1	71	64
13-week	21.3	8.7	78	78
26-week	54.9	19.9	86	83
52-week	69.4	40.2	95	89
YTD	13.6	6.1	74	83

Note: Rank is a percentile that ranges from 0 to 99, with 99 = best

Column three compares the stock's price activity with that of the benchmark S&P 500 index. It shows the percentage point differential between your stock and the index. Column four shows you how the stock performed relative to the average for the industry in which the company operates. This is a 'percentile' rank. Looking at this sample, we see that the four-week tally is 71. This means that the stock performed better than those of 71 percent of the companies in its industry. Now look at the fifth column, which contains an industry rank. It shows a percentile score of 64. This tells us that the industry performed better than did 64 percent of the industries in the Market Guide universe (viewed from a different perspective, 36 percent of the industries in the Market Guide universe performed better).

Institutional ownership

TABLE 7.5 ■ Institutional ownership

% shares owned	69.77
# of institutions	1 556
Total shares held (million)	944.064
3-month net purchases (million)	118.945
3-month shares purchases (million)	192.377
3-month shares sold (million)	73.432

Institutional ownership tables (see Table 7.5) show the extent to which institutional investors (pension funds, mutual funds, insurance companies, etc.) own a stock.

Traders take account of institutional ownership for several reasons, one of which is that if the major institutions are buying, with all their high-flying analysts backing a stock and their millions of dollars vested in these companies, then perhaps we should be more assured in our own decisions.

Other ways to use

There is another way institutional ownership can back or provide trading ideas. If institutions own a position in a small company that would indicate that the company has been noticed a little by institutions with potential for greater recognition. But the stock may rise as it gets better known and more institutions decide to buy in.

Many believe it is best to own a company that is between 5 and 20 percent owned by institutions. Such a level would suggest that there is some institutional interest and some knowledge of the company and that there's also ample room for more institutional interest in the future.

Insider trading

Who knows a company even better than institutions? Maybe the company's executives and senior officers do. These are the insiders. If they are buying then, perhaps, we should be too or at least be reassured. But it is not just their buying: their level of holding can be an important sign too.

However, when insiders own a very large and controlling percentage of the company, they may not feel responsible to outside shareholders. This is particularly visible in companies with multiple classes of stock, with insiders/management retaining voting control over the company.

Insider selling can, and often does, reflect little more than a desire on the part of key employees to convert part of their compensation (e.g. stock options) to cash for other uses (see Table 7.6). So it need not automatically be bearish. However, this is what makes insider trading a difficult gauge of a good or bad stock.

TABLE 7.6 ■ Insider trading

Net insider trades	−6
# buy transactions	0
# sell transactions	6
Net shares purchased (million)	−0.405
# shares purchased (million)	0.000
# shares sold (million)	0.405
Insider trading (previous 6 months)	

But buying by insiders could be a different story. Here, people are putting new money into the stock of their corporations and possibly reducing the diversification of their personal assets. It's highly unlikely that any insider would do this unless he/she had a favourable assessment of the company's prospects.

Of course, insiders could be buying after a big fall in the stock price in an effort to show faith in the company – and that may be a desperate attempt to encourage outsiders to invest, since, if they do not invest, it could mean the stock keeps falling. Also, insiders could simply be wrong in their assessment about the prospects of the company. Nevertheless, it is a useful indicator to take note of.

Summary

We now have a pretty good working understanding of what many professional analysts examine in companies. It also gives us some good business know-how too. Just think how many people stake their life savings without knowing the basics covered in this chapter. Scary eh? Worth a thousand times the price of the book? Well, my publishers inform me they would be delighted to take additional payment from readers – address at the beginning of the book.

But we know far from everything about fundamental analysis – that's why the book doesn't stop here. Read on!

8

More fundamentals:
this time – earnings

Wall Street is the only place that people ride to in a Rolls-Royce to get advice from those who take the subway.

Warren Buffet

In this chapter

Earnings get undue prominence from online traders as a way of generating trading ideas. Novices ask if a company is making a profit. That is too simple a question to ask when judging likely future company performance. Yet at the same time, we know from the dot.com crash that earnings are important. So now that we are confused, what should we look for? This chapter reveals how to find the most relevant pieces of information.

Objective

■ Using earnings information as a source of trading ideas.

Earnings estimates

At the end of this chapter we examine some of the best websites to find earnings-related information. You may have gathered from the previous chapter that the one I like best is the excellent www.marketguide.com – I just can't get enough of it.

Table 8.1 contains a sample of a complete I/B/E/S earnings estimates report on McDonald's. You will find reference to this in the discussion of the various components of the report that follows the table.

TABLE 8.1 ■ I/B/E/S earnings estimates report, McDonald's

Updated: 22/04/1999

Expected earnings announcements	Release date
Quarter ending 06/99	17/07/1999
Quarter ending 09/99	18/10/1999

Earnings per share estimates
Diluted EPS

	# of est.	Mean est.	High est.	Low est.	Std. dev.	Proj. p/e
Quarter ending 06/99	12	0.38	0.38	0.37	0.01	–
Quarter ending 09/99	12	0.38	0.40	0.37	0.01	–
Year ending 12/99	23	1.41	1.45	1.39	0.02	31.60
Year ending 12/00	16	1.58	1.61	1.52	0.02	28.32
LT growth rate	18	13.58	22.70	10.00	2.98	–

Analyst recommendations and revisions

	As of 22/04/1999	As of 4 weeks ago	As of 8 weeks ago	As of 12 weeks ago
1 Strong buy	6	5	NA	NA
2 Buy	8	7	NA	NA
3 Hold	7	7	NA	NA

4 Underperform	0	0	NA	NA
5 Sell	0	0	NA	NA
Mean rating	2.0	2.1	NA	NA

Quarterly earnings surprises
Estimated vs. actual EPS
Diluted EPS

	Estimate	Actual	Difference	% surprise
March 1999	0.29	0.29	0.00	0.00
December 1998	0.32	0.32	0.00	0.00
September 1998	0.34	0.35	0.01	2.94
June 1998	0.33	0.33	0.00	0.00
March 1998	0.26	0.26	0.00	0.00

Historical mean EPS estimates trend
Diluted EPS

	As of 22/04/99	As of 4 weeks ago	As of 3 months ago
Quarter ending 06/99	0.38	0.37	0.37
Quarter ending 09/99	0.38	0.38	NA
Year ending 12/99	1.41	1.41	1.41
Year ending 12/00	1.58	1.58	1.57

Earnings estimates revision summary

	Last week		Last 4 weeks	
	Revised up	Revised down	Revised up	Revised down
Quarter ending 06/99	1	0	1	0
Quarter ending 09/99	0	0	0	0
Year ending 12/99	1	0	2	0
Year ending 12/00	0	0	1	1

Note: All EPS values are reported on a diluted basis by I/B/E/S

Expected earnings announcements

Earnings release dates are very important. The run up to the announcement can be an active time for the stock. Following the announcement the stock can often move sharply too, of course. If earnings meet expectations or even exceed them, there can be a sell-off in accordance with the market saying 'buy the rumour and sell the fact'.

> *Buy the rumour and sell the fact*

A few days later the uptrend can resume as the earnings are digested by the outside community and possible positive statements flow. If the earnings estimate fails to meet expectations, we would expect the stock price to fall. However, as we note later – all is not that simple.

Conference calls follow announcements (where the company discusses results with the analysts from brokerage houses that follow the company). These too can lead to institutions' shifts in view of the stocks and announcements by them and can affect the stock price.

As important as release day is, the month or so before the release can be even more crucial. During this period, you should be alert for 'pre-announcements' that can impact stocks even more dramatically than the actual earnings reports.

> *As important as release day is, the month or so before the release can be even more crucial*

As corporate executives get closer to finalizing the upcoming financial reports, they compare their own data with analysts' projections. If there is a significant discrepancy, many will issue a written announcement (often followed by a conference call) telling the financial community that results are likely to differ significantly from consensus expectations.

The last few days before the release date are important even if there are no corporate pre-announcements, as analysts fine-tune their estimates. Increasingly large share price movements during this period, especially if accompanied by above-average trading volume, can signal changing expectations even before those changes are formally issued by the analysts. This is why your closest stock monitoring should occur in the week before release date.

Earnings per share estimates

This is where you'll find a summary of brokerage house earnings estimates for the company. The number of estimates, high estimate, low estimate and standard deviation: as you look at these remember this – a wider range of estimates means greater disagreement among analysts; greater disagreement reflects increased uncertainty; and Wall Street tends to dislike uncertainty and there may be greater stock volatility.

Contrariwise, you may choose companies for which analyst estimates are close to one another. But if such a company reports weaker-than-expected results, it will be taken by Wall Street as a harsher surprise and the stock might suffer more dramatically than would be the case if uncertainty (as indicated by a wide range of estimates) had been prevalent beforehand. There is no completely foolproof way to resolve this dilemma.

> **A diversified portfolio will reduce the risk of the inevitable earnings shock that results in a quick, sharp fall in the price of your holdings**

Remember: A diversified portfolio will reduce the risk of the inevitable earnings shock that results in a quick, sharp fall in the price of your holdings.

When studying the range of estimates, keep these points in mind:

- Note the number of analysts. A large number of analysts can add a measure of confidence to the estimates. But a smaller number of analysts can raise the possibility of a stock being a diamond in the rough; a relatively undiscovered company whose stock could perform especially well as more investors learn the story.

- Finally, you can compare these forward-looking p/e ratios to the consensus growth rate. Dividing the p/e by the growth rate will result in a PEG ratio. Many interpret PEG ratios above 1.00 (p/e ratios that are above the growth rate) as signifying stock overvaluation, but you can still use it to compare relatively 'overvalued' stocks versus each other.

Earnings surprises

You may have seen comments such as these: 'XYZ Inc. shares (XYZ – 30) lost 15 points, or one-third of their value, after the company reported first quarter earnings per share of $0.26. The result was well ahead of last year's $0.20-per-share first quarter performance, but shy of analysts' $0.29-per-share consensus estimate.'

Earnings surprises often generate rapid and large share price movements.

Look at the earnings surprise component in Table 8.1 and see what has happened over time. Years ago, when companies didn't do much to guide analysts, earnings surprises meant that the analyst was wrong. But nowadays, earnings surprises have increasingly come to mean that corporate management is wrong. And in the financial markets, few things are as bearish as a belief, among investors, that top management does not have a firm grasp on its own business.

> * Fair or unfair, earnings surprises today are perceived as company errors, not analyst errors

Fair or unfair, earnings surprises today are perceived as company errors, not analyst errors. And the simultaneous receipt of and reaction to the bad news by a large number of institutional investors sets off the selling waves that drive share prices sharply lower as soon as the news is disseminated.

In theory, the same set of reactions should occur when surprises are favourable. If one expected $0.50, couldn't one be equally leery of management's comprehension if the company reports $0.54 a share? Shouldn't the stock likewise fall in response to the favourable earnings surprise? But, in fact, this doesn't happen.

When the surprise is favourable, euphoric reaction to the traditional perception that good news will persist indefinitely wins out over concerns about company error. This is not a logical balance.

What is to be done?

The easy answer is to say you should be bullish on companies that tend to report positive surprises and bearish on companies that fall short of consensus estimates. And indeed, for many investors on many occasions, that is the correct answer. However, consider the following:

■ A lot will depend on the size of the shortfall and the range indicated by the company. If the company indicated $0.1–0.11 range and the result came in 1c shy, that may not be as bad as falling 1c short if the range were a lot more precise and the 1c fall were a larger percentage of it.

■ The vigour with which management offers its guidance will be another factor. So, check price charts and make sure the surprises that occurred in the past were actually perceived as significant by the market.

■ If a stock is pummeled to deeply depressed levels by a surprise that does not truly signal recurring trouble or management problems then that can be an opportunity to buy in.

Apple computers faced this (Diagram 8.1) when it failed to meet demand due to stock shortage resulting from a lack of semiconductors after the Taiwan earthquake in mid-September

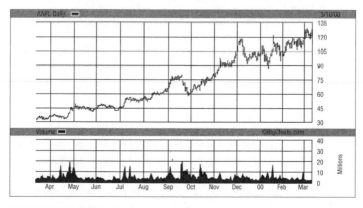

DIAGRAM 8.1 ■ Apple

1999. The stock fell some 25 percent and presented an excellent buying opportunity (a 100 percent return in six months from that point).

■ Conversely, a soaring stock price following a string of significantly favourable earnings surprises might signal unreasonably optimistic expectations that the company may be hard pressed to continue meeting. The Unisys chart (Diagram 8.2) reveals just that – the sharp drop came after a surprise earnings warning.

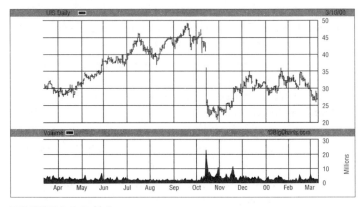

DIAGRAM 8.2 ■ Unisys

Estimates trend

The tables available from Market Guide and their explanation of their uses can hardly be bettered:

Before discussing how the estimates trend table can help you reach an investment decision, let's look at the reasons why estimates are revised:

■ Changing expectations about the economic environment: As economists raise their expectations about the performance of the economy, analysts are likely to raise their estimates of corporate EPS. The more cyclical a company's business is, the greater the likely extent of any upward EPS estimate revision.

■ The reverse, lower estimates, would occur if economists forecast a slowing in economic activity. Similarly, changes in expectations for different aspects of the economy could affect estimates pertaining to some companies.

■ For example, changing interest rate forecasts would have an impact on estimates for companies in the financial sector and other interest-sensitive businesses (such as housing); revised expectations for commodity prices would affect EPS estimates for food-processing companies and restaurants.

■ Changing expectations about a company's markets: In the late 1970s, analysts covering broadcasters devoted considerable attention to factors that were likely to influence demand for commercial advertising. That was the primary determinant of revenues (along with whatever impact inflation had on ad rates).

■ Today, even if analysts could be equally certain of their ability to estimate the dollar amount that would be spent on such advertising, they'd have other vital market-oriented issues to assess. How much of the television advertising pie would go to broadcasters and how much would go to cable networks?

■ How valuable is any television programme as an advertising vehicle considering that audiences have so many more options (i.e. can a successful network programme in 1999 hope to capture the same number of 'eyeballs' as a comparably successful telecast in 1979)? To what extent is the internet siphoning away eyeballs and ad dollars that might once have gone to network television? Etc.

As you can see, even with no changes whatsoever in economic expectations, changing markets have given analysts covering broadcast stocks many new things about which they must think and worry. Note, too, that changing markets isn't just an internet phenomenon. The political climate surrounding healthcare needs to be factored into estimates for those stocks. Increased energy efficiency has played a major role in revised earnings expectations in that sector.

Politics surrounding nuclear energy and deregulation compete with weather conditions for prominence on utility analysts' checklists of concerns and so on. The examples here show issues that have come about gradually.

But changing markets can also affect quarter-to-quarter analyst expectations. Case in point: it's reasonable to assume that retail analysts today are carefully assessing e-commerce as threats to and opportunities for traditional retailers. Indeed, at the May 1999 Berkshire Hathaway annual meeting, Warren Buffett made it clear that he's doing this:

■ Changes that are unique to individual companies: Corporate strategies change. So, too, does the extent to which management succeeds in executing business plans. New information along these lines requires analysts to modify earnings estimates.

■ Changes in how analysts assess the information available to them: As important as the three aforementioned factors are, perhaps the single most frequent source of estimate revisions is the corporate earnings announcement (or anticipatory pre-announcement) itself. However skilled and diligent members of the financial community may be, analysts can never be sure their estimates are on target.

■ And the corporate executives who 'guide' analysts toward their estimates are plagued by many of the same uncertainties that affect Wall Street. (How many banking executives truly know exactly where interest rates will go in the next quarter or year? How many retailers can say, in June, exactly how strong the upcoming holiday selling season will be?)

■ Interim earnings reports and pre-announcements are important sources of feedback that help corporate executives and investment analysts fine-tune their assessments of how the economy and various markets are performing and how much money companies will make under those conditions.

By now, it should be apparent that estimate revisions are a fact of life. You cannot reasonably expect to construct an equity portfolio that is immune to corporate earnings surprises. Instead, you should try to identify and own shares of companies that are most likely to have favorable surprises or at least avoid those that seem vulnerable to major negative surprises.

The estimates trend table helps you do this. If the table shows that estimates have been increasing over time, that means that analysts have been surprised for the better. Sometimes, the surprise surfaces in a formal manner, through an official corporate earnings release or through a pre-announcement in which analysts are guided to revise their estimates.

At other times, the surprise surfaces in an informal way, i.e. when an analyst gets information – whether from management or another source – showing him/her that estimates need to be changed. Either way, upward trending estimates show a recent history of favourable surprises. Conversely, downward trending estimates show a recent history of negative surprises (formal and/or informal).

Summary

Bear in mind that the information presented here took place in the past. One can never be certain that the future will always continue along the same lines. So there is risk/reward balancing that needs to be done. The longer a particular trend is in place, the more aggressive the stock is likely to react should that trend ever reverse. For example, a negative earnings surprise is likely to have a more dramatic effect on a company with a long history of favourable surprises, especially if the surprises are big, than would be the case had analysts previously become accustomed to receiving occasional bad news.

Earnings information does affect share prices. But it's importance depends on how highly the market regards it. Now this is where we get into a catch-22 or circular argument, because how highly the market regards the information can only be known with certainty after the event.

But there is a solution to this circularity. We can examine how much significance the market gave similar information in the past and reason that it will probably, but not certainly, do the same again. And how do we find how it behaved in the past? By experience. As time passes and our experiences increase and improve, we become better at getting a feel for how the market will respond. Our estimates become more accurate – allowing for a few errors now and again.

9

The trade planned

You can't just go out there and wildly speculate.

Bill Lipschutz, Former Global Head of Foreign Exchange, Salomon Brothers

In this chapter

A trading plan is probably the most important part of any trade. It is also the most neglected. We examine your trading strategy in brief and what planning a trade ought to involve. Then you will be able to use this in an actual trade and produce an actual trading tactic. To avoid the many pitfalls of trading we also examine keeping a journal, diversification and the types of traders that fail.

Objectives

- Learn to produce and use a trading strategy and trading tactics as part of a trading plan.
- See how to keep a journal as part of profitable trading.
- Examine the types of traders that fail.

- Look at the phenomenon of day trading.
- Understand proper diversification.

What works? Building a trading strategy

So, having examined both fundamental and technical analysis in broad outline together with some common things followers of those techniques use, you may well be tempted to ask what works. Does looking for analysts' upgrades of stock performances work? Does an examination of stock momentum work?

The unfortunate answer is that nothing works – and everything works. Nothing works, because if it did it would be consistently profitable and the puzzle of the markets would be solved. Everything works in that all the individual techniques are successful part of the time – that is why they are followed.

A guide to a DIY trading strategy

So where do we go from here? The best advice to give you is, first, read a lot more about fundamental and technical analysis from recommended reading.

Second, develop a trading strategy. A trading strategy is a set of rules which must be met before you enter a trade, as opposed to trading tactics, which are the actual specific plans for what to do once you enter a trade (discussed later).

⚡ hot tip!

Simply be aware and beware

This is a very simple guide to building a trading strategy to give you some idea of how it ought to be done. As you actually do it you will begin to realize the complexities and your plan will doubtless become more sophisticated. Every individual's trading strategy will vary and likely be unique, based on their own perspectives (see Diagram 9.1).

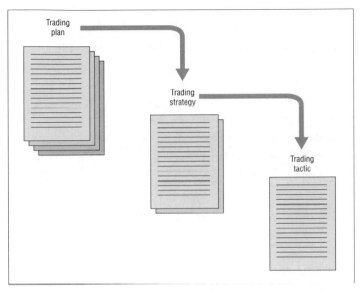

DIAGRAM 9.1 ■ The plan, the strategy, the tactic

Steps to building a trading strategy

Select some indicators

Having examined what fundamental and technical analysts commonly look for, and having done some reading about those subjects, choose some indicators you think may be potentially indicative of a rising market.

Hypothesize!

Choose some rules you consider worth testing, bearing in mind the period of time you want to be in and out of the market for each trade. Choose a target price for exit, a stop loss figure and other circumstances for exit.

> **example**

A fundamental analyst of company stocks may choose to buy a stock only if the following rules are met:

■ p/e ratio less than 7

■ analyst recommendations all being buy or higher

■ profit margin of 12 percent or higher

■ dividend yield of 12 percent or higher

■ target price: rise of 15 percent

■ stop loss: drop of 10 percent

■ exit if one of these fundamental factors changes adversely.

A technical analyst may choose stock purchase rules based on:

■ MACD crossover

■ stochastic crossover

■ rising parabolic SAR

■ a bounce off a trendline

■ target price: rise of 15 percent

■ stop loss: drop of 10 percent

■ exit if one of the above technical factors changes adversely (Diagram 9.2).

Important

Overfitting

There is a tendency when testing trading rules to 'overfit' the rules (i.e. amend them) to the data at hand so the results are good for those data only. To avoid this, do some 'out-of-sample testing', i.e. test the same rules on a completely different set of data. But beware: it may be that your trading rules do genuinely only work with that one company, both historically and in the future, and you may be throwing away a good system by out-of-sample testing. To avoid this, do some paper trades on the same stock as well (see Diagram 9.2).

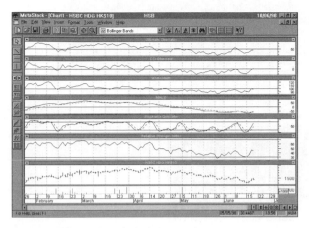

DIAGRAM 9.2 ■ A technical approach

Test

Now test the rules. Select some stocks and obtain their historical price charts. Next, see what would have happened had you used your trading strategy. What would a notional $10,000 have been at the end of one year, after dealing costs? Is the return better than bank rates of return? Did you beat the Dow or a typical mutual fund? (See Diagram 9.3.)

The preponderance of evidence rule

When testing and developing look for a balance of probability. Examine many different indicators, e.g. news stories on your product, analysts' views, market momentum. When there is a preponderance of evidence suggesting price movement, make a paper trade. Keep doing this until you are comfortable that what you are doing works. If it does not, find out what aspects do not work e.g. the technical indicators are always wrong and either amend or ditch that particular indicator.

Always paper trade with different methods of selecting trades. For instance, you may try to combine stock filters with technical indicators and plot the results together with other systems and go for what appears to make sense and is profitable.

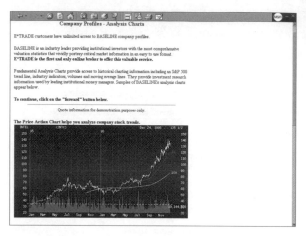

DIAGRAM 9.3 ■ Looking to buy

When you find a trading strategy you are fairly happy with you are then ready to trade.

Action plan

1 Decide if you need or want to find out more about fundamental and technical analysis.

2 Surf sites which provide analysis for your product choice.

3 Choose site(s) which you like the best for fundamental and/or technical analysis.

4 Develop a trading strategy using the guidelines provided in this chapter, then test it to satisfaction (if need be, return to Step 2 in this programme of action).

hot tip!

How to back-test well

1 I tend to test one indicator at a time and add more and more and see how that affects results.

2 Look at a chart and identify areas in which your indicators should produce signals and then find indicators that tend to.

3 Are the results very volatile, e.g. large losses and profits (even though overall profitable)? Can you handle such losses along the way?

4 Do not just test bull markets, test bear and sideways or find a different set of indicators for each type of market (Diagram 9.3).

hot tip!

Risk–reward

As a rule of thumb your upside target should be a greater percentage than your stop loss.

Action plan – creating a trading tactic

1 Using your trading rules contained in your trading strategy go through the relevant stocks, etc.

2 Select the best possibilities for price moves. Remember the preponderance of evidence rule.

3 For each possibility list the pros and cons (see Table 9.1). Select the best of the best to trade.

4 Set an upside target. What do you expect the price to reach and in what time frame? You may want to attach a rough probability of this occurring.

5 Set a stop loss – a point at which you will exit the trade: either a specific price level or a percentage.

6 Set a point at which you will sell irrespective of 4 and 5 in this list, i.e. you may get negative news on the company and decide to sell even though the stop loss has not been reached.

TABLE 9.1 ■ Part of a simple trading tactic

Pros	Cons
MACD crossover occurred	Sector undergone long bull run
Stochastic crossover	
SAR upward	
Trendline bounce	
All analysts buy or strong buy	
Sector strong	

The mind of a trader

Stick to your plan. Do not start hoping for price moves or denying losses. Try to keep objective. Do not get attached to a position: each day is a clean slate. To learn more about trading plans and trading like a professional you might consider reading *The Mind of a Trader* (Pearson Education, 1997).

Journal keeping

I am regularly asked by traders what they can do to improve their trading. One of the easiest and simplest steps that can be undertaken is to keep a journal. Imagine all that information and experience you collect as you trade. Without a journal you are throwing so much of it away. Without a journal you are in serious danger of repeating your mistakes. In this regard, keeping a journal is a money and risk management technique. By identifying possible trading problems, you can start to resolve them. So, make journal keeping a goal.

> ✱ *Without a journal you are in serious danger of repeating your mistakes*

What to record

1 You will want to have a copy of your goals and note your progress in achieving them.

2 *The anatomy of every trade*: Write down, from the moment you started analyzing a stock to the moment after you sold it, how you felt at each key moment about every activity you undertook. You may want to compare that with what you know about how you should have reacted, in light of what you have read in this book. For example, how did you feel as you approached your stop loss?

3 Write down what feels good and what feels uncomfortable about what you are doing.

Remember to keep your notes clear and well presented. You will have to return to them at a later date.

Trading types

There are many types of trader. An awareness of the varieties when looking at your trading plan allows you to avoid the pitfalls.

Disciplined

This is the ideal type of trader. You take losses and profits with ease. You focus on your system and follow it with discipline. Trading is usually a relaxed activity. You appreciate that a loss does not make for a loser.

Doubter

You find it difficult to execute at signals. You doubt your own abilities. You need to develop self-confidence. Perhaps you should paper trade.

Blamer

All losses are someone else's fault. You blame bad fills, your broker for picking the phone up too slowly, your system for not being perfect. You need to regain your objectivity and self-responsibility.

Victim

Here you blame yourself. You feel the market is out to get you. You start becoming superstitious in your trading.

Optimist

You start thinking: 'It's only money, I'll make it back later.' You think all losses will bounce back to a profit or that you will start trading properly tomorrow.

Gambler

You are in it for the thrill. Money is a side issue. Risk and reward analysis hardly figures in your trades; you want to be a player: you want the buzz and excitement.

Timid

You enter a trade, but panic at the sight of a profit and take it far too soon. Fear rules your trading.

10

Money and risk management for e-trading

- How much of my money should I risk on a single trade?
- How much money do I need to start online trading?
- What sums have other successful online traders started with?

Money management is about as exciting as a date with an actuary. Unfortunately for online traders, it is also essential to understand if we are to play the game and make money. Consider the simple fact that if you suffer a 50 percent loss, it will then take a 100 percent return just to break even. Not a nice prospect is it? That's why you shouldn't leave home without money management.

In this chapter

In this chapter we run through some of the mathematics of money management. It complements the later chapter on the psychology of risk and money management. Don't worry, you won't need a calculator.

Calculating how much to risk

Now, this may seem a bit detailed and tedious, at least that is what I thought when I first realized years ago that it was important. However, if you are serious about making money from trading then you just have to take another sip of the gin and tonic and read on.

Whether a trade is worth making depends on the risk to reward levels, not just on the signals your system provides. By risk I do not mean the size of your position, but the size of your potential loss.

Imagine you are trading one contract of the FTSE future. The same principles apply whatever product and time frame you are trading. Each point equals £10 per contract (£10 = $16 approximately). Imagine you also have £10,000 to trade with in total capital. Your reasoning should run like this:

- How much of my total equity should I be willing to risk? Most experts would advise anything from 0.5–5 percent of your total equity per trade.

- In this case since you have £10,000 in total equity, the most you should be willing to risk in one trade is £500.

- £500 is 50 points movement (remember each point is £10).

- So, the maximum number of aggregate points I can afford to lose is 50. (I have said aggregate because if you trade one contract it would be 50 points, but if you trade two it would be 25 points on each and so on).

- Now imagine that the contract is at 6580, you expect a move to 6610. That is a profit of 30 points per contract (see Diagram 10.1). There are now two considerations: For a good trading system your downside should be determined by your expected upside. So, if you are expecting 30 points on the upside, you should *not* be willing to risk 50 points on the downside to achieve it. What should the upside to downside ratio be? Well, 2:1 at least. So the most you should be willing to risk, given an upside of 30 points, is 15 points on the downside, i.e. downside stop of 6565. That is good risk and money management. So your risk to reward ratio is 1:2. But how many contracts should you have?

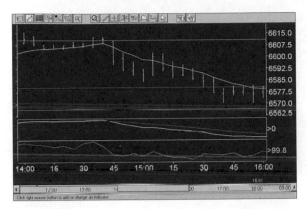

DIAGRAM 10.1 ■ FTSE future contract with price at 6580

■ You can afford to have three contracts because even if you lost 15
points on each that would total 45 points, which is less than 50.
So in that situation you would buy three contracts, and still limit
your downside risk to 5 percent of total equity on the trade with
a 2:1 reward to risk ratio. Wasn't too painful, was it? Now, how
about a whisky?

Let us just run through that again:

1 Five percent of your total equity determines the most loss in
aggregate you can allow yourself to suffer on a trade. In this case
it is 50 points in aggregate. Of course, you could limit it to 3
percent.

2 Your downside risk has to be at least half that of your projected
upside reward. Upside points gain is estimated to be 30 points,
so your downside can only be 15 points.

3 You can afford to have three contracts each losing 15 points and
still have maintained your equity loss to under 5 percent.

So, what happens? (See Diagram 10.2).

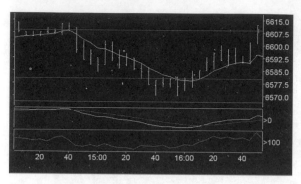

DIAGRAM 10.2 ■ FTSE 100 future

As you can see, from our entry point the future did move down a little bit, but not so much as to activate our exit, and then moved towards 6610 just as we anticipated and hey, presto! – 30 points per contract, three contracts, that's £900 pounds total profit or 9 percent return on total equity, in a few minutes. Remember we had limited calculated risk. Don't you just love it?

(i) *expert advice*

Bernard Oppetit, Global Head of Equity Derivatives, Paribas

You have to have good money management. You have to ensure you are not going to be hopelessly underwater. You can have rules like maximum drawdown, or value at risk, or limits. You can also have your own internal rules like 'this is too much money to lose'. You must have that in your mind and that you are not going to risk more than that at any one time. You have to make sure you are left in the game. That is very important. Once this is clearly established, you need fear, you need to feel that things can very quickly go wrong.

chat box

From a trader on Silicon Investor on 6.6.1999
The figure of merit is how much of your equity is at risk for each consecutive trade. The book suggests that 1 percent is a reasonable figure. This applies to the amount at risk, not the gross amounty of the trade. For instance, if you could relatively expect to scalp a reasonably liquid stock without ever having a loss worse than $3/4 per share, then in order to trade 1000 shares, you would need to have $0.75* 1000/0.01 = $75,000 in your account.

example

It is not necessarily a risky business
Imagine you risk 2 percent of your equity in any one trade. Allowing for the fact that your account size drops on each occasion, your initial equity would be down 50 percent after 34 consecutive losses. What are the chances of 34 consecutive losses? Well, if there is a 50–50 chance of profit on any one trade then the chances of 34 consecutive losses would be 0.5 (3/4) or one in 17 billion. Makes you wanna trade doesn't it?

What if you limit the most equity you are willing to lose on a trade from 5 percent to 3 percent?

In this case, you would reduce your overall risk to 3 percent, but you also reduce the number of contracts you would be trading, so if the trade were profitable your rewards would be reduced. By reducing your risk, you protect your downside more.

What if I am willing to accept a 1:1 reward to risk ratio?

The upside would be that you would give the price more room for manoeuvre, i.e. allow the trade more space to prove itself; the price could drop further before you had to exit. But the downside is that if the price just kept falling you would suffer a bigger loss when you exited. Another risk is that you are not playing the odds and if you got a string of losers you could be wiped out.

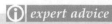 *expert advice*

Bill Lipschutz, former Global Head of Foreign Exchange, Salomon Brothers

With a trade you always look at a multiple upside to downside. But how much greater? A good rule of thumb for a short-term trade – 48 hours or less – is a ratio of three to one. For longer term trades, especially when multiple-leg option structures are involved and some capital may have to be employed, I look for a profit to loss ratio of at least five to one.

 chat box

The loser's spiral – the dark side of trading

From a trader on Silicon Investor on 9.6.1999

All of us, as traders, normally sense that trading can become 'dangerous', if you let it get out of control when it's not going well. It can indeed be a rather dangerous (risky) endeavour, financially speaking. A friend of mine, after trading marginally successfully for a few months, said to me: 'Man, I sense this is really dangerous – I could get into a lot of trouble here.' He was right. There is one basic process that destroys almost everyone that 'blows out' of trading; I call it 'the loser's spiral'. I know all about it, as I went through it myself several times, in the process of really learning how to trade more consistently. Only extreme interest in trading, and perseverance through travails got me through this one! I've never met a good trader who hasn't been through grappling with this, either. As they say: 'You must learn how to lose before you can win.' It is 'the filter' which keeps most away from full-time, long-term trading success.

It goes something like this (simplified for brevity). Trader makes a bit of money. Skills develop. Trader makes a lot of money. Trader takes bigger risks. Things going well. Then ... Wham! Big loss. Wham! Bigger loss. Trader tries to 'make back' loss by taking bigger risks ... and so on. The spiral is self-perpetuating.

Think that won't happen to you? Well, it happens to 80 percent of beginning traders within six to nine months (mileage varies depending on prevailing market conditions). It happens to a lot of intermediate traders and experienced traders. It happens to world-class traders who run huge hedge funds and it happens to people that have written scholarly books (Victor N.) and who are geniuses.

So don't think it can't happen to you – it will, unless you study the mathematics of money management and carefully calculate how much you can risk, versus your total tradeable capital. The statistics are overwhelmingly against you, if you violate the cardinal rules (generally, if you are risking more than 1–5 percent per trade, depending on your trading style). For those with higher net worth, more tolerance for risk or a longer time frame (usually a combination of these factors), the parameters are different. But the basic idea is, if you are trading too 'large' (of risk on each trade), sooner or later it will destroy you and blow you out of the game – probably sooner rather than later.

Other factors to consider

Market volatility

The price could be moving about so greatly that the place where you have to put your stop to prevent your losing more than 5 percent of your equity is just too tight and is likely to be hit. In that case you cannot place the trade. It is too risky.

The upside might also be so small that you have to have a tight stop loss and again it may have to be so tight that it would be easily hit and would not be worth your time (see Diagram 10.3).

If you anticipated a price move from 105 to 110, i.e. a 4.8 percent upside, your downside protection would have to be at most 2.4 percent, i.e. at 102.5. As you can see, such a tight stop would be hit in normal daily volatility. The trade is just not worth it. This is actually an extreme example, but the principle is the same.

Of course, when you first put on a trade you do have target levels, levels at which you think you are wrong. The price levels of those targets should be determined as a result of your absolute dollar loss constraints. For example, let's assume that the current price level of dollar yen is 125 yen per dollar. Let's further assume that your analysis of the latest round of trade negotiations between Japan and the US leads you to believe that the yen may

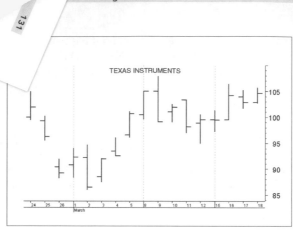

DIAGRAM 10.3 ■ Lone Star Instruments

(i) *expert advice*

Bill Lipschutz, former Global Head of Forex, Salomon Brothers

With a trade you always look at a multiple upside to downside. You can look at the percentage probability of a rise or a fall. The problem with that is that you may have many trades that are 50–50. So you are trying to set something up which may have a 8:1 payoff. The fact of the matter is that if you put a lot of 14:1 structural ratio spreads, you are going to make money, because you have to be wrong 14 times in a row to lose, for every once you are right.

I think risk is asymmetrical. To achieve successful longevity, you have to focus on your losses, or drawdowns or whatever you call them. It's very simple. Just know what you are prepared to lose. It doesn't matter how big, little, right or wrong your position is. You have to know what you are prepared to lose; I don't mean mentally prepared, I mean mathematically what can be lost when you enter a trade. You must not put yourself out of business. You have to be back. You have to be there tomorrow, the next day and the day after. If you manage the downside, the upside will look after itself.

weaken to 130, but due to technical considerations should not strengthen beyond 122.50.

Further analysis of the pricing of yen options leads you to determine that the optimal trade structure will be simply to sell the yen against the dollar in the spot market. How large should the position be? The answer lies in the asset size of the account you are doing the trade for and its loss limit. If you are only prepared to take a 3 percent loss on a 10 million dollar account, then it follows that you should buy $15,000,000 against the yen. If you are wrong on the trade, your loss will be $300,000 and if your analysis was correct and you sell the position at 130, your profit will be $500,000.

Probabilities

Strictly speaking, you should calculate your reward to risk ratio based not just on absolute figures but expected profit and expected loss. What does that mean? Well, let me give you some (painless) probability theory first.

Your expected gain is the probability of the gain occurring multiplied by the value of the gain. Trust me, this is relevant to trading. So, imagine there is a die. If it shows 1–5 I will lose $5, but if it shows 6, I will win $30. Should I take the bet? Trading the markets is a little like this.

In this example, my expected gain is $1/6 \times \$30$ i.e. $5 (i.e. the probability of a 6 on a die is $1/6$). My expected loss is $5/6 \times \$5$, that is $4.17. So, since my expected reward is greater than my expected loss, I should take the bet.

Of course, I will lose more times than I win, but when I win, I should wipe out my accumulated losses. You could have a trading system that produces $30 profits one-sixth of the time and $5 profits five-sixths of the time. But note that your reward:risk ratio would not be 30:5. This is very important. If you forget the probabilities of your system, then you will think you are placing more favourable a trade then you actually are.

Doing the maths

So how do you calculate the probability? You could use sophisticated computers or back-test your system and estimate. Remember, even in a game of dice, there are no guarantees, only theory and reality and they seldom converge. Large price moves have a lower probability of occurring than smaller ones. My suggestion is not necessarily to be hyper-scientific, but to take probabilities into your calculations.

During the inevitable 'learning curve' virtually all traders lose money. The tough decision is when to 'pull the plug' and give up

 expert advice

Bernard Oppetit, Global Head of Equity Derivatives, Paribas

Even though I know I will get out after a certain loss, I consider the amount I have risked as the whole amount invested. Also, I look to see what percentage probability there is of a certain percentage rise and I compare that to the risk I am taking. I would look at some kind of distribution of possible outcomes, such as 50 percent chance of doing something special, or a 50 percent chance of doing nothing in particular, or a 50 percent chance of a small loss against a 50 percent chance of a great gain. There has to be some idea of the distribution of outcomes.

 chat box

When should I quit?

From a trader on Silicon Investor on 6.6.1999

Successful trading is very difficult. The vast majority of those who try day trading end up losing money. However, the few successful day traders make huge sums of money – once they gain the knowledge and experience to be successful.

day trading if you are not successful. The following ideas may be worth considering:

■ Are you financially secure enough to trade without the anxiety of needing a 'pay cheque' at the end of every day?

■ Does day trading still interest you? Do you look forward to the open of the market every day? In short, do you enjoy trading? If not, you're likely not committed to the extent that is required. Most people cannot excel at something they don't enjoy. The most successful people are virtually immersed in their fields.

■ Is your trading improving? If you have made several hundred trades, you should be seeing some improvement in your trading results. Keep detailed records of your trades in a spreadsheet. This will give you irrefutable data that show your results in black and white. Don't argue with the facts.

■ In addition to the statistical data, do you feel you are avoiding many of the dumb mistakes that you made when you first began trading?

■ Are you trying to trade with some kind of plan or are you just trading from the seat of your pants? Hopefully, after several weeks or months of trading, you are beginning to formulate some ideas on personal trading strategy to guide your trading. Even if not successful with a particular strategy, you will gain knowledge by *learning* that the strategy was not successful. Then you can modify or refine your system to improve performance. If you trade by the seat of your pants, you have no reference point to *what* you were doing that was unsuccessful.

> *Do not let your ego prevent you from giving up trading*

The decision to quit trading is a very difficult one. Over 90 percent of day traders wish they had made this decision sooner. Do not let your ego prevent you from giving up trading. The odds are stacked extremely heavily against success. People who lose money are in very good company. Not being a successful day trader should be nothing to cause embarrassment or to be ashamed of.

In the end, it is a personal decision of when to stop day trading if you cannot find success. I think an individual needs very honestly to review their situation and make their best decision.

Note: Don't decide during market hours!

 *expert advice*

Jon Najarian, CEO, Mercury Trading

I believe discipline could be a learned response. You could teach somebody to do it, but you really have to hammer it into them if they have got a problem – you cannot let them ride it at all. You have to be very, very honest with yourself. The single biggest thing is that they need to have a goal for every trade that they make. So if I do a trade and, say, I am buying a stock at $30 because I think it is going to $35, then I know what my downside limit is; it is $25, because if I am going to make $5, if I am right, then I do not want to have to lose more than $5 if I am wrong. So if I have a goal which I think the stock is going to reach, then as a minimum I set my loss at where I think the gain could be if I am right.

How much money to start with?

A very popular question raised by many new traders is how much money they should start trading with. Well, the answer is not as simple as giving a figure. You didn't think it would be, did you? Consider the rich trader and the poor trader.

Rich trader

This trader has oodles of cash, let's say $1,000,000 for argument's sake. His problem is not whether he has the minimum needed to trade, but rather: 'What is the minimum he should trade with?'

Just because you have a small fortune does not mean you should look to use it all in your trading. It is advisable to paper trade first, then trade small and gradually build your way up as your confidence rises. The issue of how much the rich trader should start trading with depends on his answers to the following:

- How confident do you feel?
- How much trading experience do you have?
- Have you traded this product or time frame before?
- How profitable have you been so far with the system you plan to use?

The other problem the rich trader has is one of opportunity cost. Does he really want to use all $1million trading a system producing 20 percent return a year? He may be better placing some money into other ventures.

Poor trader

This trader is more like most of us. He does not have a silver spoon in his mouth or any other orifice for that matter. Consequently, he is wondering whether he has enough money to trade with at all. The first thing to bear in mind is that if you trade with money that is needed for other more pressing things, such as school fees, mortgage, clothing, food, then pretty soon you will lose it. You would simply be putting too great a strain on yourself to 'perform' to succeed. You should be trading with 'uncommitted' funds.

The minimum needed to trade with depends on the following factors:

- Those listed in the 'rich trader' section you've just read.
- Broker account minimums:
    - These are so low nowadays they are not too large a hurdle.
- The volume of trading you are intending to do:
    - If you are planning to day trade, that means you will be expecting to make a lot of small profits daily. So you will be trading high volume each day and incurring commission for each trade.

Of course, the optimist will argue that he will reinvest all the profits he intends making back into his trading account. In which case, he may calculate a shorter time frame than a year as a benchmark for profits. For instance, commissions for a month of day trading on the trading in our example is $3333.

Whatever happens you would have to have enough money to make $3333 profit a month, just to break even.

The key point is that the lower the volume of trading, the less trading capital you need:

■ Profits to make the endeavour worthwhile: If your system was likely to produce 100 percent a year return before commissions, then in the first month you may expect 9 percent return before commissions.

■ To improve your profit, you can either: increase your trading capital, your system's return or reduce commission costs by trading less while maintaining returns.

 example

If you trade ten times a day and pay $8 to open and $8 to close a position and trade 250 days a year, then you will pay $40 000 in commissions.

example

If you had trading capital of $50,000 then at the end of the first month you would have 2.3 percent return for the first month after commissions (using our previous example of ten trades daily at $8 to open and to close).

That would equate to 28 percent annualized *after* commissions *without* reinvestments of profits – or $14,000 in profit for the year (before tax).

That is not much of a return for a lot of hard work *and* that was with a system producing 100 percent a year.

chat box

Minimum trading money for day trading

From Eric P. of Silicon Investor 6.6.1999
While different traders may disagree on this point, I believe that $50k is about the right minimum size for a day trading account. Anything less can reduce your likelihood of success ... and the odds are not great to begin with.

 chat box

Minimum trading money for day trading

From Palo Alto Trader on Silicon Investor on 17.6.1999
I would say $50,000 is rock bottom to have decent odds. $75k is OK, $100K is a good number, not too big, not too small. I've day traded and swing traded $25k and $50k accounts at times in the past myself.

Below $25k, I'd recommend instead of trying to day trade, swing trading positions to build up the account. It can be done! You just have to be really cautious, since there is less margin for error.

Understanding risk

I would rather underperform and have a better risk to reward ratio than be a star performer taking great risks. Trading is not a one-shot game and in the long term I would be the outperformer.

Even those who have some idea about risk, use outdated, unsophisticated or discredited measures. Beta is a popular yet incomplete measure of risk. Beta measures how much an individual stock is likely to move with the general market.

> *I would rather underperform and have a better risk to reward ratio than be a star performer taking great risks*

A beta of 1 means that a stock will tend to move lockstep with the general market, while a beta of 2 means that the stock will rise 2 percent for any 1 percent rise in the stock market and fall 2 percent with any 1 percent fall in the stock market, on average.

But beta can be misleading. For instance, because two stocks with the same beta generally have a different level of risk. Standard deviation is another common measure of risk and it too has deficiencies. For example, it fails to weight historical share prices to give more significance to the most recent prices.

New online tools remove traditional problems with risk measurement. This will potentially result in greater online trading returns. JP Morgan have taken their internationally and institutionally acclaimed RiskMetrics risk calculations and converted them for the private investor through RiskGrades (www.riskgrades.com).

This is a very powerful tool. It reveals, for instance, that Moulinex and Intelek are equally risky (in very simple terms they have been equally volatile in the past six months), yet the one-year returns are –35 percent and 115 percent respectively.

RiskGrades also suggests online traders have riskier stock portfolios than they realize. Consequently, their returns are often lower than they expect – losses greater than anticipated or profits lower than they should be.

> * Since risk and diversification go hand in hand, how many stocks should a well-diversified portfolio contain?

I suggest the serious private investor should know the following about their stock portfolios: which stocks contribute the greatest risk to their portfolio; how well diversified their portfolio is; what you should expect to see as an average worst case one day trading loss; whether replacing any stocks reduces risk without impacting return or even improving it. Use RiskGrades to evaluate these for your portfolio.

Since risk and diversification go hand in hand, how many stocks should a well-diversified portfolio contain? As few as a dozen stocks can yield good diversification. A diversified portfolio is one where the negative impact on a portfolio of an event due solely to a specific stock is minimized.

But all important in diversification are the stocks you select. Again, too many private investors have stocks closely correlated to each other. Simply buying a stock from different sectors is not

* **Too many private investors have stocks closely correlated to each other**

the answer for sectors can be linked in their movements too. RiskGrades allows quick assessment of how diversified your portfolio is.

The trick with a portfolio is to maximize reward for any level of risk through asset allocation. According to RiskGrades an aggressive portfolio can produce an expected annual return of 30 percent, but that is only if the assets are allocated to minimize risk.

Unfortunately, many traders first select risky 'growth' internet stocks, reasoning that if they are risky then growth will follow. Such fallacious reasoning is equivalent to saying: 'Producing high-grade steel results in pollution, so if I pollute, I will produce high-grade steel.' Consequently, they have all the risk, but little of the return because of the assets selected.

Once again the online tools of RiskGrade assist in resolving that problem.

Too few private investor websites understand online trading. If they did they would provide as much statistics about risk as they do about p/e ratios. Doubtless brokers will provide such information with the motive of encouraging greater trades as investors re-jig their portfolios in pursuit of the ideal portfolio.

E-traders need to beware there is the risk of overtrading and incurring commission costs for themselves

* **E-traders need to beware there is the risk of over-trading**

from doing so that is not measured by RiskGrades.

Bear in mind one further piece of risk advice from JP Morgan, actually, *the* J. Pierpont Morgan: 'The market will go up and it will go down, but not necessarily in that order.'

Summary

If there were just one essential secret to trading then money management and limiting the amount you risk on any particular trade would be it. It is a question of getting the numbers on your side. Pay great heed to this chapter.

11

Eyes and ears open:
monitoring

It takes a lot of patience and energy and motivation.

Bernard Oppetit Global Head of Equity Derivatives,
Banque Paribas, discussing trading

In this chapter

Having executed your position after analyzing numerous possibilities, monitoring your open positions and positions you may
open is a key part of any trader's time. In this chapter we examine
what you monitor, when and why and how it fits into the overall
trading approach

Objectives

- Understand the importance of portfolio monitoring.
- Examine how the internet can assist in the task.
- Further add to a professional approach.

Monitoring what?

Traders monitor:

1 What they own in anticipation of the time when they will want to sell according to their trading plan.

2 Possible other products they may buy but for which as yet all the factors they look for are not quite aligned, e.g. the price may not be too high or too low as yet.

3 The price of the product.

4 In the case of an open position, all the fundamental and technical factors which led to the decision to buy and are contained in the trading tactic.

5 In the case of a potential position, all the fundamental and technical factors the trader usually examines as part of the trading strategy before entering a position.

> *Monitoring involves a constant re-analysis and revaluation of a position to see what has changed

In other words, monitoring involves a constant re-analysis and revaluation of a position to see what has changed.

Monitoring when?

How often you monitor depends mainly on two things:

1 Your trading strategy time frame: Are you looking to enter and exit in a short, medium or long period of time? Table 11.1 should help.

2 How close is the position to your stop or target? The closer it is the more regularly you need to monitor.

How the internet assists

Numerous sites have portfolio monitors or trackers. These usually relate only to stocks. Diagram 11.1 shows a typical portfolio. These are helpful in that you can see all the details for your stock in one place. Most update the price and volume of your stock.

TABLE 11.1 ■ Suggested monitoring time frame

Period expecting to enter and exit	Monitor
24–96 hours	Constantly – hourly
1–2 weeks	Twice during day monitor price; end of day monitor everything else
1 month	End of day monitor price; every 2 days monitor everything else
3–9 months	3–4 days monitor price; every week monitor everything else
9 months +	Monitor situation every 3/4+ weeks

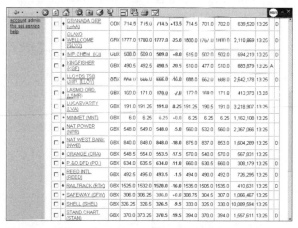

DIAGRAM 11.1 ■ Online portfolio monitor

What to look for when seeking an online portfolio tracker

- Does it recalculate the value of your total holdings?
- How many stocks can you list in one portfolio?
- How many portfolios can you have at one site?
- How often is the portfolio updated?
- Does the portfolio tracker alert you about news, earnings or other related items which may affect your stock?
- Does it monitor and alert you to a change in the technicals of your stock?

Summary

We have now examined what a professional approach to trading requires in terms of monitoring open and potential positions:

- With both the trading strategy and the trading tactic in hand, monitor both the open and the potential positions.
- Frequency of monitoring depends upon how close the target or stop is and, generally, on how quickly we expect to enter and exit.
- Portfolio monitors exist which can help reduce the workload.

12

Essential trading psychology for online trading

As part of my endeavours to discover the traits of the leading traders in the world and what they can teach the rest of us, I interviewed Bernard Oppetit, former Global Head of Equity Derivatives at Paribas. This part of the interview focuses on risk and money management – two essential components to trading success.

Great traders tend to be risk averse

The public perception of traders, propagated by trading scandals, is that they are attracted to wild risks and take massive gambles. Of all the traders I interviewed for this book, not one claimed to be risk loving.

Oppetit details the contrary view:

I am very risk averse. I would definitely take the certainty of making $10,000 than the 10 percent chance of making $100,000. In terms of economics, my personal utility function is very much concave.

When we speak of risk in trading we are, of course, discussing price volatility. Price volatility cannot be discussed without an idea of probability. The probability of a stock's price reaching your target can be derived from the historic price volatility of the particular stock. Consequently, risk, price volatility and probability go hand in hand. Good traders wait until the probability of a favourable move is the greatest and the risk of an unfavourable move the lowest. Moreover, unlike non-professional traders, the great trader knows that risk and reward are not always directly proportional. There are very low-risk and yet high-reward trades.

> ✳ **When we speak of risk in trading we are discussing price volatility**

Oppetit continues:

The important thing is to look at risk in a rational way and an imaginative way. A good trader knows how and when to take risk and how and when to avoid risk. There are risks which should be taken and risks which should not be taken. The game is to distinguish between the two. You do not need to risk a lot to profit a lot. There are a lot of trades where you can make a lot of money which are not particularly risky. You may have to invest a lot of your time to do research and discover what is going on, but the actual money you invest may not be at much risk.

There is a joke about an economics professor who is walking in New York with a friend. His friend notices a $100 bill on the sidewalk and points to the bill and says, 'Look professor, a $100 bill.' The economics professor replies, 'No that can not be so, if that was a $100 bill somebody would have picked it up already.' Still I believe there are opportunities to make money with very little risk.

Analyzing risk and probability

So, how does Bernard Oppetit analyze risk and probability when he examines a position?

Even though I know I will get out after a certain loss, I consider the amount I have risked as the whole amount invested. Also, I look to see what percentage probability there is of a certain percentage rise and I compare that to the risk I am taking. I would look at some kind of distribution of possible outcomes, such as a 50 percent chance of doing something special, or a 50 percent chance of doing nothing in particular, or a 50 percent chance of a small loss against a 50 percent chance of a great gain. There has to be some idea of the distribution of outcomes.

What Bernard Oppetit does when analyzing a potential trade is to consider at risk the whole amount he is trading with. This is even if he knows that he will exit the position if the price falls by, say, 15 percent and, therefore, he would risk losing only 15 percent of his stake.

He then examines the reward. He measures reward by examining the probabilities of various outcomes. You can only gain an idea of the reward if you examine the probability of its occurring.

Bernard Oppetit would then compare the risk with the reward. For instance, an options position opened with $10,000 would place $10,000 at risk. To get an idea of his risk and reward ratio, Bernard Oppetit would then examine the likely outcomes and their probabilities. This would give him some idea of the reward he may get for the risk he is taking. (If he were being very mathematical he would sum the products of all the outcomes and their corresponding probabilities, and compare this figure to the amount risked.)

Money management

Good risk analysis and management is not only about volatility and probability, it is also about good money management.

As Oppetit explains:

You have to have good money management. You have to ensure you are not going to be hopelessly underwater. You can have rules like maximum drawdown or value at risk or limits. You can also have your own internal rules like 'this is too much money to lose'. You must have that in your mind and that you are not going to risk more than that at any one time. You have to make sure you are left in the game. That is very important. Once this is clearly established you need fear, you need to feel that things can very quickly go wrong.

In devising a money management plan, you should consider the following:

- What is the most money I will risk on any single trade at any one time, i.e. what is too much to be lost?

- What amount must I avoid losing on a trade, given that I might lose on a consecutive number of trades, so that I do not become in serious danger of being out of the game?

- Once in the trade, what is the maximum percentage I am prepared to lose before exiting? Some decide this based on 'value at risk', i.e. a mathematical calculation based on the probabilities of various outcomes of all open positions and hence the value of money at risk of the positions.

Facing a loss

When sitting on a paper loss a trader will indubitably experience immense pressure and fear.

Oppetit continues:

It is very important to experience this fear to ensure you do not end up in that situation again. Fear is also a bad thing in that it will affect your judgment, in the same way elation would affect your judgment. You have to take a very neutral approach.

So, experience the fear when faced with a loss, do not deny it. But use the fear as a means of loss prevention in future, not as a cause of ever-increasing losses. When looking at a new price you do not focus on the fear of how much you have lost or the hope it may turn around:

You have to ask, if you are a buyer at this new price, if you didn't own it already, would you buy it? If the answer is no, then I sell it. You have to look at the position with an open mind and ask if you would put it on today if you did not already have it. If new information came in while I had an open position, I would change my expectations. But you have to be honest with yourself. It is a question of attitude. It is an easy trap to fall into to kid yourself that you are holding onto something because you believe things have changed and it will now rise. It comes back to being honest with yourself.

Handling a profit

As well as hope, another damaging emotion surrounding open positions which prevents an honest analysis, is that an unrealized profit may vanish:

It is a cliché that you cut your losers and ride your winners – but it is very true. Most people and many traders do the opposite. There is a desire to take profits, sometimes encouraged by accounting rules. Many people look at their unrealized gains as non-existent. They think taking profit is making real profit and it is unreal before then. They feel taking a loss is an admission of being wrong.

Again, this emotional attitude to profits has to be eradicated.

Instead of focusing on whether he was right or wrong, Bernard Oppetit focuses on his expectations regarding a position, in order to maintain objectivity:

If what I had expected to happen does not happen then I know to get out. Whether I get out at a profit or loss does not matter. As soon as I realize my scenario was wrong I get out. Another easy case is when everything I expected happened, so I take my profits. Those are the two easy cases, and everything in between is difficult.

What Bernard Oppetit is discussing is that all open positions have to be viewed objectively. That means you have to focus on certain questions and reasons and ignore others.

You need to focus on these points:

- Has what you expected to happen happened?
- Are you a buyer or a seller at this price?
- Is the probability of what you expected to occur still the same as when you placed the trade?

You have to ignore:

- How much of a loss you are sitting on.
- How much of a profit you are sitting on.
- How much you paid for the position.
- The fact that the position may turn around.

advice from Pat Arbor

Risk taking is older than literature. As far back as 3500 BC the *Mahabharat*, the holy scriptures of the world's oldest religion, Hinduism, describes a game of chance played with dice on which kingdoms were wagered. Little wonder then, as Peter Bernstein states in *Against the Gods* (Wiley, 1998): 'The modern conception of risk is rooted in the Hindu-Arabic numbering system that reached the West seven to eight hundred years ago.'

Dealing with risk is part and parcel of being a trader, and many traders great and small will have their own ideas about risk management. But what precisely is the relationship of the great trader to risk? What would an experienced trader such as Pat Arbor, former Chairman of the Chicago Board of Trade, the world's largest derivatives exchange, have to say about risk?

Risk: Why take it?

'Nobody ever achieved greatness by doing nothing. You have got to step out and do something and take a chance and get your teeth kicked in. A good trader has to engage in some acts which are considered risky,' says Arbor.

As Pat Arbor explains great traders take risks and manage risks:

I think a great trader certainly has to have a psychological stability about themselves, but not too much stability, because one has to have a

> **I think a great trader certainly has to have a psychological stability about themselves**

certain flair for risk. It is a fine psychological blend you have got to look for in a trader; the ability to take risk, the ability to have some courage, coupled with stability in the psychological make-up. I think the great traders have to have a greater appetite for risk than the normal person or the poorer traders. Then the question is how they manage that risk, the discipline they impose on themselves to manage that risk.

In most cases the risk is balanced. In my own trading I have always tried to be a spreader or arbitrageur. If I am long one month soybeans then I am generally short another month soybeans. And I generally do soybeans or bond spreads. If I am long bonds then I am short 10-year notes. Sometimes if I am long a commodity outright, then I might be long corn and short soybeans or long soybeans and short corn.

You also spread because you may not be prepared for the straight position. You may like the position, you may be bullish on the position and it may not be going well. You would like to maintain your position, possibly moderate it a little, by selling something against it. You may be long soybeans outright and you can neutralize it a little by selling soybean meal or soybean oil or some corn against it. Your S&P position may not be going so well and you may want to sell bonds against it. You are keeping your position but cutting your profit potential.

Of course, you could just take the loss. But where you may not do that and have a spread instead is where you think you are right and like the position then you tend to neutralize it a little bit to mitigate the loss.

Spreading or hedging as a form of risk management is not necessarily suited to everyone, as Pat Arbor explains.

Finding a style to fit

As a trader you must decide what you are. You are either a speculator, spreader, or local scalper. You have to fit into one of those categories. Me, I am suited to spreading.

To find what suits his personality, he just has to see whether or not

> *To find what suits his personality, he just has to see whether or not he makes money at what he's doing*

he makes money at what he's doing. I have had people come into the office, saying, 'I am a great trader', I say, 'You're right', they say, 'Know how to trade'. I say again, 'You're right' and they say, 'I predicted that the market was going to go up or down', and I say again, 'You are right. But the bottom line is whether you make any money.'

So, while hedging can be a good way to manage risk, whether or not you wish to be a hedger depends on what trading style makes money for you given the type of trading personality you are.

From small acorns: progressive trading

Progressive trading is the name I have given to the idea that the best trading results and long-term profitability are assured through a 'slow and steady' style of trading. I have yet to meet a great trader that advocates wild risks in order to make spectacular home runs.

As Pat Arbor continues:

The best traders I think are those who try to make a little bit every day. You surely have your success stories; those that hit home runs, but if you take a record or study of the home run hitters against those that try to hit singles every day, the success rate of the former is a lot less than

> **The best trading results and long-term profitability are assured through a 'slow and steady' style of trading**

the latter. So a good trader ends up being one who accumulates capital over a period of time.

I remember once explaining this to a young Italian trader and I said to him, it's una fagiola (one bean) a day. If you try to put one bean in a bag per day, then at the end of the month you are going to have 31 beans in the bag. But if you try to put all 31 beans through the mouth of the bag you will spill a few and in some cases you will not get any of them in. So, it is better to build it up one day at a time, in a small manner, slowly. It's tempting not to do that when you see George Soros, but if you live by the trading sword, you die by the trading sword.

Implicit in Pat Arbor's advice about 'progressive trading' is the idea that it is all right to be out of the market:

> **The discipline not to trade, that's a big one**

The discipline not to trade, that's a big one. A lot of people don't realize that. A lot of people think you should stand there all day long and be in the market all day long. There are times when the market is so dead or so illiquid that

you should not be trading. There are times when the market is terribly volatile and makes no sense and you should not be trading. It is generally the former, though. I have seen people stand there all day long when there is nothing going on, just a few locals in the pit. They will put a position on out of boredom. Then they can't get out of it easily. I say to them, 'Well, you shouldn't be trading. There's nothing going on. Take it easy. Take a walk. Go off to the coffee shop.'

I think I'll go for a coffee right now.

Risk aversion: Risk not thine whole wad

Trading is about risk. Risk can be bought and sold like any other commodity. Derivatives are one instrument through which risk is

> **Trading is about risk**

transferred. The great trader has a deep understanding of the nature of risk, but, perhaps most surprisingly, is risk averse; he takes out insurance against being wrong. Moreover, he balances risk with his own personality to produce a harmony between the two; never being so exposed as to feel uncomfortable and let it affect his trading.

Six feet tall, a muscular physique and bald save for a ponytail – that is Jon Najarian by appearance. In 1989 Jon Najarian formed Mercury Trading, a designated primary market maker, responsible for maintaining a market in stocks for which it had been designated. Two years later, it reported a return on capital of 415 percent. Today it is the second most active market maker on the CBOE.

As he is a highly profitable trader, I wanted to know what he would have to advise other traders about risk.

Perceptions of trading risks

As Najarian explains:

I am very risk averse. You have probably seen on people's walls: 'Risk not thine whole wad.' We always try to position ourselves so that we can always trade tomorrow. That is the single most important thing. Not making money today, making money today is not more important than being able to come back tomorrow. If I want to be short the market, because I think they are going to raise rates and that will pressure the market, will I be naked short? No, we are long puts and every day that goes by and the market drops, we buy a ton of calls so that if the market turns and goes up we do not lose all the money that we made by being right. You only get so many times a year to be right. But we always want to lock in the profits so we are constantly rolling down our hedge and never just one way long or short. Many days when placing a spread or a hedge, we think: 'God, if someone had tied me up in a closet we would have made a fortune, because as the stock was falling we were taking profits all the way down.' Well that is just the curse of being a hedger. It is also the reason why we sleep the way we sleep every night.

Because Najarian knows he has disaster protection insurance, he can be more at ease:

When you come in after a weekend where the market was down 148 points, it looks ugly, they were having trouble finding buyers all day, then if I am stuck in a position I could be very panicked. But we sleep like babies.

Any temptation to go for home runs?

It is comforting to know that the top traders have the same bad trading temptations as the rest of us:

Sure, there are times when we wished that we were not as disciplined. But more times than not we were glad that we were disciplined. We see so many people bet for home runs by putting all their marbles on a big shot. When we bet on a big move we do it with a controlled amount of risk even though we are betting for a home run. We are buying a lot of out-of-the money puts and we are selling out-of-the money puts as well as a hedge against the puts we are buying. If we say we are buying some puts for $4 and selling other puts for $2 then we only have $2 worth of risk. So I can stay at the table twice as long. The other guy, who is unhedged, is starting to gag when the market is going against him, but we can stay with the trade longer.

> **When we bet on a big move we do it with a controlled amount of risk even though we are betting for a home run**

Since the hedge provides Jon Najarian with a comfort zone, he can be free to exercise clearer judgement. Imagine the last time you were panicked by an adverse price move. Did it ruin your day? Did it plague your mind? Did it affect other trading decisions? If so, have you considered hedging your position? You will, of course, have to examine the cost elements of hedging and the extent you may wish to be hedged. Risk is a beautiful thing, with ingenuity you can purchase or sell just the precise amount of risk:

The other thing we look at is the buyers and sellers. Again, on the derivatives side we see Salomon, Morgan Stanley, Lehman, NatWest buying, buying, buying a certain stock and we know they are betting on the upside, too. So, we are reading all these tea leaves as well. We see that the chart pattern looks good, institutional buyers are coming in – is there anything in the news? Are there earnings coming up, has anybody commented on it favourably, is there a new product coming out, is there a lawsuit pending? We look at all those things so that by the time we actually place the bet we probably have a huge edge because of all those factors we looked at, that our winning percentage is off the charts. Most people do not have the benefit of seeing all that information so what they have to do is give themselves the chance of being as right as possible.

> **So, we are reading all these tea leaves as well**

It follows from this that when Jon Najarian does enter a trade he wants the upside to be far greater than the downside, even if the downside move is highly improbable:

The worst I do is a 1:1 risk reward ratio. Most of the time I want a 2:1 or 3:1 reward to risk ratio. So if I think it could go to $35 then I sell at a loss, if I am wrong at $29 or $28 so that I have a multiple risk reward ratio on the upside. If I am wrong I cut the trade and move on.

You cannot be willing to say I am going to ride this stock down to $20 if I am wrong, but I am going to make $5 if I am right. If you do that kind of thing you are just not going to be in business very long.

I would never put a multiplier on the risk to the downside. I would never say that although there is $5 on the upside, I am so confident that I am willing to take a $10 risk to the down side. It would not be acceptable risk.

Few people would associate such a risk-averse, belt and braces approach with a trader, let alone a great trader. However, risk aversion and caution are the hallmarks of great traders. While many of us may have a strong appreciation of this, it can never hurt to be reminded.

The equation using other people's funds

Many traders dream of going it alone and managing money. So what are the pitfalls that a private trader working for himself should be aware of when competing against the institutions?

Bill Lipschutz is an institutional investor who went it alone and set up his own company. Lipschutz was Global Head of Currency Trading at Salomon Brothers at the end of the 1980s. If ever there were a right time and a right place for a trader, that was it – then and there.

Over the eight years he was there, Bill Lipschutz earned for his employer an average of $250,000 profit each and every trading day. Here is a man who knows his trading.

It's not all the same money: Source and effect

Bill left Salomon in 1990 and currently has a company called Hathersage Capital Management, focusing on FX Trading.

It is often not realized that the source of trading funds can affect one's trading style and performance. As Bill Lipschutz explains, this fact is something even the most able traders do not appreciate until they experience it:

I was unaware that there were these differences. Seven years ago, I had a naive view that you get the money from here, or from Salomon Brothers' proprietary capital, whether it is ten high net worth individuals or a fund of funds I felt it was all the same; let me see how much I can extract from the market.

The whole money management game is a difficult game. It has not only to do with how well you perform, but what kinds of results people are looking for in their portfolios. Absolute performance is a real

> **Absolute performance is a real misleading thing**

misleading thing. I can say to you, 'We were up 600 percent' over five years in our most aggressive program, and you might say, 'wow, 600 percent'. But that does not necessarily mean that much in and of itself, without knowing how well other currency-only managers performed. For example, say a guy is managing $200 million, and $120 million of it is a fund that he runs with a very specific mandate. If he made 600 percent over four years in that particular fund, he may have people pulling money out from that particular fund, because they are nervous, because that really was not the kind of variance they were looking for. So, it is very complicated.

As Lipschutz explains, one way the source of funding can affect your trading style is through the motivation of the lender and the terms on which the funds were granted. We all, as traders, seek more capital with which to trade. Whatever the source of money, you must be aware that since it can affect your trading style it may

> **The worst time to have a deterioration in your trading performance is when the money is not your own**

also affect your trading performance. The worst time to have a deterioration in your trading performance is when the money is not your own:

But, now when you have to charge clients, the client says to you: 'I know you are a speculative guy or you can be a speculative guy, I am willing to lose 20 percent.' I have sat with clients and we try to talk with our clients and really understand what they want. If a guy looks me in the eye and says, 'I can be down 20 percent, no problem,' I know he really means 5 percent, because if you call him in three days and say, 'You know what, you're down 18 percent, I just wanna know how you feel, so we can discuss what to do from here,' he's going to forget he ever said he was comfortable with a 20 percent loss.

Regardless of what they say, because they are not traders, they don't understand, they certainly do intellectually, I am not trying to take anything from them, but they don't understand it emotionally, necessarily, what they are getting into. When you are charged with other people's money you have to help them and not let them get into something they are not emotionally ready for yet.

Sometimes, being wrong, even if there is a 5 percent chance of that happening, is a whole lot worse than being right, even if there is a 95 percent chance of that. It's the old: 'Gee, if I make 25 percent for these guys, they'll be really happy, and they'll think I am a great trader and I'll earn big fees. But you know what, if I lose 5 percent for these guys they're going to pull that money out and I am going to be close to being out of business.' But that is not the probability of the trade succeeding or failing. So you have to lay this on top of the probability of the trade succeeding or failing. It is very complicated. It's a whole set of simultaneous constraints that you have to solve at once.

> ✳ **Sometimes, being wrong, even if there is a 5 percent chance of that happening, is a whole lot worse than being right, even if there is a 95 percent chance of that**

Therefore, trading with other people's money becomes far more complicated than with one's own. You have to consider both the likely outcome of the trade and the likely reaction of the investor to a positive and a negative trading outcome. The decisions you can make are restricted by the likely responses of your client. That, in turn, could impinge on your trading performance.

So, before taking on new funds, run through the following checklist questions:

1 What does the lender *say* he expects?

2 What does he *really* expect?

3 Have I traded successfully in the past *in the manner required* by the lender's expectations?

4 Can I *deliver* what the lender really expects?

5 What are the consequences for me if I *fail* to deliver?

6 How much *control* does the lender want?

7 How *frequently* is the lender going to inquire about the performance?

8 What type of *personality* has the lender? Is he likely to pester and aggravate?

9 Can some *ground rules* be set?

Something new, something exciting: universal stock futures

Online trader problems

■ I want to spread my wings with something a little bit sophisticated and something that gives the opportunity of big gains.

Universal stock futures – what are they?

A universal stock future is a contract, in fact futures are sometimes referred to as 'contracts'. But unlike buying shares now at a given rate, a futures contract means one party undertakes to buy shares at a future date at a price fixed now.

When seen for the first time, futures prices can seem odd. Each futures delivery month of the four available has a price which is different from each other delivery month *and* different from the price of the underlying share. Have a look at Table 12A.1 as an example:

TABLE 12A.1 ■ Universal Stock futures

Bid	50.00	50.19	44.99	50.19	50.80
Offer	50.05	50.25	50.05	50.26	50.87
Stock					
January future					
February future					
March future					
June future					

Buying a universal stock future is similar to agreeing to buy shares at a future date, but agreeing the price at the time of trade. The key difference is that universal stock futures are cash settled, so no shares change hands. Conversely, selling a universal stock future is similar to agreeing to sell shares at a future date (although the seller does not need to own shares to enter into this agreement).

Both the buyer and the seller face a risk that the share price changes between the date the future is traded and the end of the futures life. To cover this risk, the seller of the future could buy shares and hold them until the future's last trading day.

The futures price should be equal to the cost of buying the shares and holding them until the expiry of the futures contract – any more and a trader buying stock and selling futures would make a guaranteed positive return – any less and a trader selling stock and buying futures would make a guaranteed positive return. If a futures price were to move away from the correct theoretical price, the process of buying/selling stock and selling/buying futures, usually referred as *arbitrage* would bring the price back in line.

Assessing the total cost of buying stock and holding it until the expiry of the future may seem difficult to anticipate but it is really made up of three main elements:

1 the price of the underlying stock

2 any interest income foregone by holding shares rather than cash

3 any dividends paid to the holder of the stock before the expiry of the future.

There is, theoretically, a formula for testing the fairness of a futures price:

$$\text{Fair futures price} = \text{today's share price} + \text{Interest costs} - \text{Dividends received}$$

However, the normal forces of supply and demand operate just as much on LIFFE's universal stock futures as in any other market

* Stock futures are capital efficient

and prices are subject to fluctuation. Equally important, each investor will have his own set of priorities leading to an individual set of expectations as to what constitutes a fair price for a future.

A stock future is, quite simply, an agreement between a buyer and seller to exchange cash at a fixed future date (the settlement date) reflecting the difference between the initial traded price and the price of the stock on the settlement date.

An investor can benefit from a predicted rise or downward move in the stock price by buying or selling a futures contract respectively. For instance, buying one stock future contract of Vodafone at 230p represents 1000 shares. So a change in the future's price to 231p as the stock rises means a return of £10.

Stock futures are capital efficient. The capital needed is the amount of margin payable, freeing capital for other investments.

For instance, in the example trade it may cost £2290 to buy 1000 Vodafone shares excluding commissions and stamp duty. To gain the same exposure one would buy only one Vodafone stock future contract. Since one pays margin the capital cost would possibly be around £230.

Another advantage of stock futures is that they offer a single access point to some of the most actively traded stocks in the world, including Nokia, France Telecom, Deutsche Bank, ING,

Cisco, Intel, Microsoft, and major UK stocks including Vodafone, HSBC and AstraZeneca.

However, although new stock futures were to be added throughout 2001, at launch there will be stock futures on only 25 stocks.

The greatest advantage of stock futures is their versatility. If a trader is of the opinion that the stock market is going to fall, a trader can sell a contract. A profit will be made if the trader then buys that contract back later when the price decreases. This will be useful in 2001 as Morgan Stanley Dean Witter recently reported that they foresaw a 45 percent chance of a global recession. The rebuttal by Merrill Lynch only serves to highlight the advantages of a product flexible enough to profit from market rises and falls.

Their flexibility allows the sophisticated online trader to make precise bets about stock movements. For instance, believing that Vodafone will outperform Deutsche Telecom, you can buy Vodafone and sell Deutsche Telecom stock futures.

> *Their flexibility allows the sophisticated online trader to make precise bets about stock movements*

Portfolio hedging is a by-product of stock futures flexibility. Perhaps you own 1000 Vodafone shares and feel for the month ahead the stock is going to drop, but longer term is a good investment. Rather than selling your entire stock holding for that month then incurring stamp duty in buying them back, you could sell short 1 Vodafone stock future contract (which represents 1000 shares) for the month. If you change your mind mid-month, cut your loss and buy the contract back.

The main benefits of universal stock futures

The great thing about universal stock futures is that it makes equity trading available to a wider audience and offers greater efficiency and liquidity to the underlying market.

Another factor to bear in mind is that it sidesteps many of the difficulties faced by investors attempting to trade across jurisdictional boundaries by providing access to UK, European and US shares on a single trading platform.

> The great thing about universal stock futures is that it makes equity trading available to a wider audience and offers greater efficiency and liquidity to the underlying market

Essentially, the benefit can be summarized as direct, hassle-free access. The electronic trading system used, LIFFE CONNECT™, is currently available to around 14,000 traders and 366 different companies, in 23 countries around the world. This means ordinary investors will have access via the internet.

Cost savings

There is no stamp duty to pay with futures on UK stocks. This means lower transaction costs than cash equity transactions. Universal stock futures transactions will be clear of costs of accessing settlement systems across international borders.

The overall savings are considerable when trading futures rather than shares. Trading futures is around one-third the cost of trading shares.

Lower capital outlay

Traders can make big upfront capital savings. Compared with trading on the traditional cash market, there's a reduction in capital required upfront because the trader is only required to pay margin upfront with stock futures.

Typical margin required by the London Clearing House is approximately 7 to 15 percent of contract value, depending on volatility of stock.

Therefore capital investment amounts only to the margin payable, which frees up capital to pursue other investments.

Enhanced performance

Traders can profit no matter what direction the market moves in.

If a trader is of the opinion that the stock market is going to fall, a trader can sell a contract. A profit will be made if the trader then buys that contract back later when the price decreases. Avoids the hassle of stock borrowing.

They also allow investors to switch exposure from one stock to another without disturbing the underlying stock holding.

Universal stock futures can be bought and sold more easily than shares – as futures do not require cross-border settlement and the trade is cleared by the London Clearing House.

Just some of the major stock futures

Stock futures, as you can see from the partial list below, are on major blue chip companies, listed on the major exchanges.

Key to list

1 Stock

2 Country

3 Domestic stock exchange

4 Category

5 Market cap 20 Apr 2001 (bn)

ABN AMRO Holdings NV
Netherlands
Euronext Amsterdam
Banks
34

Aegon NV
Netherlands
Euronext Amsterdam
Insurance
50

Alcatel SA
France
Euronext Paris
Technology
40

Allianz AG
Germany
Deutsche Börse
Insurance
77

American International Group Inc.
USA
New York Stock Exchange
Insurance
209

Amgen Inc.
USA
NASDAQ Stock Market
Technology
65

AOL Time Warner Inc.
USA
New York Stock Exchange
Media
229

Assicurazioni Generali SpA
Italy
Borsa Italiana
Insurance
45

AstraZeneca plc
UK
London Stock Exchange
Pharmaceuticals
93

AT&T Corporation
USA
New York Stock Exchange
Telecoms
95

Axa SA
France
Euronext Paris
Insurance
56

Banco Bilbao Vizcaya Argentaria SA
Spain
Bolsa de Madrid
Banks
50

Banco Santander Central Hispaño SA
Spain
Bolsa de Madrid
Banks
50

Barclays plc
UK
London Stock Exchange
Banks
58

Bayerische Hypo- und Vereinsbank AG
Germany
Deutsche Börse
Banks
33

BNP Paribas SA
France
Euronext Paris
Banks
45

BP plc
UK
London Stock Exchange
Oils
229

Bristol Myers Squibb Company
USA
New York Stock Exchange
Pharmaceuticals
125

British Telecommunications plc
UK
London Stock Exchange
Telecoms
56

Carrefour SA
France
Euronext Paris
Retailers
47

Cisco Systems Inc.
USA
NASDAQ Stock Market
Technology
124

Citigroup Inc.
USA
New York Stock Exchange
Banks
280

DaimlerChrysler AG
Germany
Deutsche Börse
Automobiles
56

Deutsche Bank AG
Germany
Deutsche Börse
Banks
55

Deutsche Telekom AG
Germany
Deutsche Börse
Telecoms
84

E.ON AG
Germany
Deutsche Börse
Technology
43

EMC Corporation
USA
New York Stock Exchange
Technology
92

Enel SpA
Italy
Borsa Italiana
Technology
45

Eni SpA
Italy
Borsa Italiana
Oils
62

Exxon Mobil Corporation
USA
New York Stock Exchange
Oils
344

France Telecom SA
France
Euronext Paris
Telecoms
90

General Electric Company
USA
New York Stock Exchange
Technology
549

GlaxoSmithKline plc
UK
London Stock Exchange
Pharmaceuticals
185

HSBC Holdings plc
UK
London Stock Exchange
Banks
131

ING Groep NV
Netherlands
Euronext Amsterdam
Banks
75

Intel Corporation
USA
NASDAQ Stock Market
Technology
216

International Business Machines Corporation
USA
New York Stock Exchange
Technology
225

JDS Uniphase Corporation
USA
NASDAQ Stock Market
Technology
27

Juniper Networks Inc.
USA
NASDAQ Stock Market
Technology
18

Koninklijke Ahold NV
Netherlands
Euronext Amsterdam
Retailers
28

Koninklijke Philips Electronics NV
Netherlands
Euronext Amsterdam
Technology
41

Lloyds TSB Group plc
UK
London Stock Exchange
Banks
66

Marconi plc
UK
London Stock Exchange
Technology
15

Merck & Co., Inc.
USA
New York Stock Exchange
Pharmaceuticals
193

Microsoft Corporation
USA
NASDAQ Stock Market
Technology
414

Münchener Rücksversicherungs Gesellschaft AG
Germany
Deutsche Börse
Insurance
56

Nokia OYJ
Finland
Helsinki Exchanges
Technology
160

Olivetti SpA
Italy
Borsa Italiana
Technology
17

Oracle Corporation
USA
NASDAQ Stock Market
Technology
106

Pfizer Inc.
USA
New York Stock Exchange
Pharmaceuticals
301

Qualcomm Inc.
USA
NASDAQ Stock Market
Technology
49

Royal Bank of Scotland Group plc
UK
London Stock Exchange
Banks
69

Royal Dutch Petroleum Company
Netherlands
Euronext Amsterdam
Oils
144

Shell Transport & Trading Company plc
UK
London Stock Exchange
Oils
93

Siemens AG
Germany
Deutsche Börse
Technology
69

Sun Microsystems Inc.
USA
NASDAQ Stock Market
Technology
58

Telecom Italia Mobile SpA
Italy
Borsa Italiana
Telecoms
79

Telecom Italia SpA
Italy
Borsa Italiana
Telecoms
63

Telefonica SA
Spain
Bolsa de Madrid
Telecoms
84

Total Fina Elf SA
France
Euronext Paris
Oils
123

UniCredito Italiano SpA
Italy
Borsa Italiana
Banks
26

Vivendi Universal SA
France
Euronext Paris
Media
84

Vodafone Group plc
UK
London Stock Exchange
Telecoms
215

Volkswagen AG
Germany
Deutsche Börse
Automobiles
19

Wal-Mart Stores Inc.
USA
New York Stock Exchange
Retailers
257

How do they compare to other similar products

Table 12A.2 shows you.

TABLE 12A.2 ■ Universal stock futures compared to similar products

	Universal stock future	Equity spread bet	Equity contract for difference
Description	Contract where participant gains/loses difference between the opening traded price and the final closing price set by LIFFE on a pre-determined date	Bet where participant 'wins' or 'loses' change in value of shares at a predefined future date	Contract where participant gains/loses difference in equity value between opening and closing the contract
Price determination	Standard futures pricing model operated by each market participant – best prices determined on LIFFE CONNECT™	Standard futures pricing model used to determine value, but not price competition to determine best market price	Traded price equal to prevailing share price. An additional financing cost is imposed on CFD positions

	Universal stock future	Equity spread bet	Equity contract for difference
Liquidity	Competing quotes on LIFFE CONNECT™ supported by market makers	Volume is 'guaranteed by spread but firm exit price is an uncertainty	Acces to market is 'guaranteed' by counterparty
Expiry date	Yes	Yes	No
Settlement style	Cash settled	Cash settled	Cash settled
Final closing price	Determined by the exchange based on underlying share price	Determined as per terms of the agreement	No automatic closure – closing price established as prevailing share price at closing trade

Summary

This appendix has covered the basics for those already familiar with computers and the internet. Most entry-level PCs will accommodate all the aspects mentioned here and you will not have much to worry about. People with older systems may need to upgrade, however.

13

Top trading psychology tips from leading traders of the world

This chapter contains a list and summary of the main traits the leading traders exemplified.

Since kindergarten each of us is taught to grab our opportunities for they do not knock twice. It is precisely that type of advice, which is so useful in other walks of life, that is detrimental in trading.

Many traders, armed with their trading plan or strategy, will often hastily and prematurely enter a trade. Their decision is often driven by fear; the fear of the missed opportunity. Their mind will be screaming: 'Quick get on the trade, you're going to miss it, so what if all your criteria for entering a trade have not been met? Most of them have, so get on, the big traders wouldn't hang around.'

The inevitable result is that the trade will not be profitable or not as profitable as it would have been had the trader waited for the precise moment to strike.

In trading the fear of the missed opportunity leads to many avoidable losses. And the game of trading is as much about avoiding losses as about capturing profits. The leading traders have a different perspective on opportunity.

Counter-intuitively, they know opportunity knocks once, twice and then kicks the door down. They know that if this trade does not feel absolutely perfect, there will be another one along in a short while that will. That knowledge alleviates and overrides any fear. That knowledge is the key to unlocking greater profits by waiting for all the trade entry criteria to be met and not cutting corners.

Bill Lipschutz summed it up when he said:

Out of 250 trades in a year, it comes down to five, three of those will be wrong and you will lose a fortune and two will be right and you will make a fortune; for the other 245 trades – you should have been sitting on your hands.

Luck: stacking the odds

Following on from the nature of traders as being risk averse, they have a knack for stacking the odds. As Lipschutz puts it: 'I happen to believe that by far the biggest component of trading success is luck, it's not the rolling the dice type of luck, but stacking the odds.' These top traders practise their risk aversion by ensuring the odds of a successful outcome are heavily stacked in their favour.

This is not only done by ample research and planning, but also by recognizing, when they *are* in a good trade, to 'push their luck'. As David Kyte, Chairman of the Kyte Group and the largest local on LIFFE put it: 'You do not step in the way of a train that's going at full steam.' Najarian and Kyte both said: 'You make your own luck in this game,' meaning that you stack the odds of making a profitable trade by planning and waiting until all your trade entry criteria are satisfied, if then the trade does prove to be as lucrative as it promised you 'push your luck' by perhaps adding to the position and riding it for all it is worth.

The emotional problem

Traders' attitude to their potential and existing positions is often a great determinant of success. As every trader knows, the moment a trade is executed, everything is different. That is the point at which it becomes real, no longer digits on a screen and numbers in an account. Now expectation is joined by anticipation. The brain is joined by the heart. Reason is joined by emotion. You exchange detachment for attachment.

> *The moment a trade is executed, everything is different ... you can exchange detachment for attachment*

When you have an open position and you are looking to close it, you will either have a profit or a loss. The emotions relating to each are quite different. For instance, when sitting on a loss many traders experience hope that the position will turn around because they fear and deny that it may not. It is for you to recognize these emotions and to discard them. Your judgement has to be based on detached reason relating to your analysis of the company.

How you behave once you have an open position is all important. Without clear thinking, you could exit too soon or too late. Your key concern with an open position is timing your exit.

> *An open position requires an open mind*

Of course, there are times when you are deciding whether to add to a position, but generally you are concerned with exit. With an open position you are concerned with closing the position. In order to do that an open position requires an open mind.

As Oppetit puts it:

The key is to be intellectually honest. You have to think of every day as a clean slate. You've got to forget about your loss or how much you paid, you have to treat each day as a completely new day. You have to start every day with a blank page. Mark to market should be the rule so you start each day afresh. There is no expected profit or loss on the book so you have to start from scratch each morning.

P**s poor planning produces pathetic performance

Although an SAS motto, this statement is equally applicable to trading. Top traders do not trade 'by the seat of their pants'. Planning and its benefits are a key aspect to the way they view the markets. The top traders plan 'what if' scenarios and think about their response to each probable outcome. The main benefits are that with plan in hand or in mind the trader's confidence is enhanced, fear of loss reduced and that in turn assists clear thinking and removal of hope so ensuring the trader stays focused on his original reason for entering the trade.

Oppetit summed this up well when he said: 'Whether I get out at a profit or loss does not matter.' Martin Burton, founder and Managing Director of Monument Derivatives and former director of NatWest Markets was talking about the same thing when he said: 'It is not a 90-minute game.' They both know that sticking to their plan is far more important than temporary blips in their profit and loss accounts.

Losses: a curious view

The top traders are totally at ease with losing. This is not something one expects from those at the top of their profession.

> ✳ **The top traders cut their loss and move on**

Although true in other walks of life, that perfection is to be striven for, in trading perfection is not an option. Paul RT Johnson, Vice President at ING Securities and a director on CBOT said bluntly: 'You are going to be wrong. You are not perfect.'

The top traders cut their loss and move on. The issue is not whether the market may turn around if they hang in there. They cut their loss if it is what they say they will do in their plan. They get out at the predetermined level. The discipline of sticking to the plan is primary and the real issue. To say 'cut your losses short' misses the whole point and is of no help to anyone. By cutting their loss they can free up capital to place in more profitable positions elsewhere, and free up mental energy to focus on new opportunities. Pat Arbor summed it up by saying: 'Your first loss is your best loss.' Jon Najarian has a saying as to why cutting losses was so important: 'You can't eat like a bird and s**t like an elephant.'

Summary

It is not possible to do justice to the wisdom and accumulated experiences of the world's leading traders in a short chapter. However, I have tried to convey how their minds work in a way that apparently runs against common intuition. These differing perspectives ensure that with the same tools and products to trade with as anyone else they make far more in profits because their minds are different.

14

Chats and boards

- How best to use online chat sites, if at all?
- Which are the key sites online traders use to talk trading?

The aim of this book, as with all good trading books, is to impart more than information. Its aim is also to impart knowledge and wisdom. The experience of others besides your humble, yet omnipotent, author is essential to such a task. In trying to maintain a community feel boards and chat rooms are an essential source of information, making this an important chapter in the book.

A top chat room or board will create a genuine community feel with intelligent conversation, inclusive of all experience level users. Unfortunately, such chat rooms are as rare as a Democrat president who doesn't philander.

With a chat room you can talk real time by typing, posting, and seeing instant replies (if anyone is in the room and deigns to reply). With boards you post a message and wait for a reply at some future time. In this chapter we shall see some of the 'best' ones, what 'best' means and how to use them.

Why and how they are used

- To pose questions about issues you are unsure of.

- To get ideas about what to trade. Be very wary of using them for this. A lot of posters put the 'bull' into 'bulletin board'. Be especially concerned if anyone offers insider information: it is usually the last cry of someone stuck in a bad losing position.

- As an educational tool by learning from the experiences of others, for instance in which orders to use at what time of day.

- As a review of online trading sites. By this I mean many postings may review who are the best brokers, the cheapest sites etc.

- Just to 'chill' and bond!

chat box

From Sam on Silicon Investor

- Getting a read on a general market perception.

- Getting a heads-up on stock movements you are not following that day (i.e. momentum trades).

- Feeling out on others' thoughts on particular stocks, sectors, news releases etc.

- Companionship.

But it is not good for getting picks in real time, imo.

That said, know your fellow posters. There will be those you trust and those you don't. Most, unfortunately, are not to be trusted. Not that they are looking to screw you, but more likely (as with SI) they will only admit selective info. Thus, it goes without saying, don't ever follow the hype. Remember, if someone has made a move, you are already too late for the party. Don't allow yourself to buy their shares as they corral you into a foolish move. You are not in the business to bail them out. But, if you *can* trust them, you can see what they are

> **❋ Getting other people's picks should never be a priority**

playing on any given day and why. But don't let it rule your day. That's just plain lazy. It is a learning tool – that's all. There's work to be done all day long. Research and analysis (as well as actual trading). Getting other people's picks should never be a priority.

Glossary

You will need to know the first terms just so you too can appear dead cool by knowing what the board's hippest in-crowd is talking about. It's a sociological thing (see Diagram 14.1).

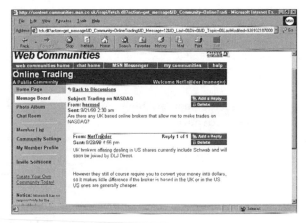

DIAGRAM 14.1 ■ Hip talk

B4	before
BBL	be back later
BCNU	be seeing you
BFN	bye for now
BRB	be right back
BTW	by the way
CUL8R	see you later
F2F	face to face
FAQ	frequently asked questions
FWIW	for what it's worth
GBH&K	great big hug and kiss
HHOK	ha ha, only kidding!
IMHO	in my humble opinion
IRL	in real life
J/K	just kidding!
LOL	laughing out loud
NT	no text
NTR	not trading related
OIC	oh, I see!
OTOH	on the other hand
OTT	over the top
ROTFL	rolling on the floor laughing
TIA	thanks in advance
TTFN	ta-ta for now

Before I set you loose, you will also need to know the following.

Flaming

A nasty or rude response to someone who breaches netiquette, e.g. by posting adverts, thereby treating the board members like buffoons.

Posting

The act of placing a comment on a board, done by a poster.

Thread

This is a line of discussion on a board with one person making a posting, the replies being the threads. Also, a thin piece of material used to keep garments together.

What to look for and watch out for on chats and boards sites

When considering which chats and boards sites to make your regular hangouts, you should consider the following issues.

Size

When it comes to boards, size matters. You obviously want a board with lots of subject matter and members to ensure you get the broadest views and are not sharing the site with a sad lonely broker from Florida.

Quality of postings

Some sites just have poor-quality postings for several reasons. It may have been taken over by a few 'bully' posters who cajole, intimidate or just try to poke fun at anyone who may not know as much as the bullies think they themselves do. Sometimes postings are poor because the people posting on them are simply not that good and postings degenerate into slanging matches and challenges to settle matters outside the board. Sometimes you get an invasion of ramping postings: those morons who inform you something is about to skyrocket because they know a man, who works for this woman, whose husband's mistress's cousin's niece's stepmother's alien dog told her the stock was a good purchase.

> * *When it comes to boards, size matters*

Topics

As well as a wide range of topics the boards should be divided into subgroups so you can get into a relevant topic in enough detail and quickly.

Design and navigability

It can sometimes seem that there are millions of messages on billions of topics posted every nanosecond. In fact, it is worse than that. All this makes design and navigation especially important otherwise you will never get to read about what you want to know or post questions or replies.

Price

Ideally, you want a free site. Failing that a free trial period followed by a cheap subscription will have to do.

15

Speeding things up

In this chapter

We examine some quick tips which may help tune up your computer and squeeze that extra iota of performance out of it and the browser.

Objective

■ Learn some quick ways of speed surfing.

Speed surfing

Clear cache

The sites you visit are stored on your computer's hard disk. To speed things up when downloading web pages you can:

■ In Internet Explorer (Diagram 15.1) click on the View drop-down menu and then on Internet Options; on the General tab click on Delete Files and on Clear History.

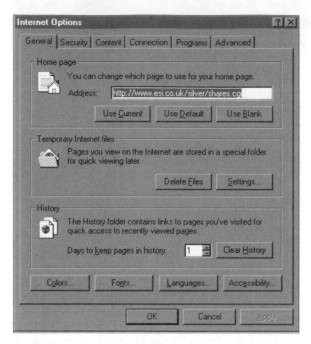

DIAGRAM 15.1 ■ 1E4 with Options folder open

■ In Netscape Navigator (Diagram 15.2) click on the Edit drop-down menu and go to Preferences and Navigator, then click on Clear History; under Advanced go to Cache and then click on Clear Memory Cache and Clear Disk Cache.

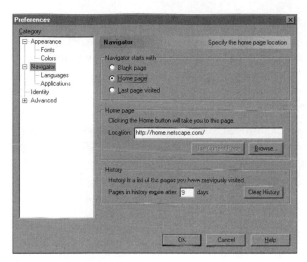

DIAGRAM 15.2 ■ NN4 with Preferences folder open

Turn off graphics

Pages load a lot faster if you are not downloading graphics:

■ In Internet Explorer 5 click on the View drop-down menu and then on Internet Options; on the Advanced tab scroll down to Multimedia and clear the Show Pictures box.

■ In Netscape Navigator click on the Edit drop-down menu and go to Preferences and under Appearance click on Text Only.

Open multiple windows

Remember you can launch multiple copies of your browser simultaneously, so while surfing one page you can wait for another to download.

Time your time online

Internet speed slows down around 7–10am EST (US) and 4–7pm EST (US) when internet traffic is horrendous. Browse around 3am EST for best results!

Increase cache size

Pages you have visited already are saved on your hard disk and loaded from there before being downloaded by your browser if you visit them again. Since downloading from a cache is quicker than from the internet you should increase the size of your memory cache:

■ In Internet Explorer click on the View drop-down menu and then on Internet Options; on the General tab click on Settings and adjust size of cache.

■ In Netscape Navigator click on the Edit drop-down menu and go to Preferences and Advanced and then Cache and Increase size.

Defrag

Downloaded web pages get scattered around on your hard drive, which means your computer gets slower and s-l-o-w-e-r at finding them from the cache. Defragment your hard drive to reduce this and speed things up.

In Windows click on Start then on Programs; next go to Accessories, then System Tools and Disk Defragmenter.

Summary

There are various things you can tweak on your browser to make things happen a little faster. We have explored them in this chapter. Most internet magazines, and the help files in browsers, usually contain a good splattering of tips and tricks too.

Quotes sites

Some killer quotes sites

These are my picks of the bunch and how I use them, as well as their strengths and what not to use them for.

ADVFN***
www.advfn.com

How to use it and what for
Excellent web site offering wide-ranging trading facilities including free real time streamed quotes. Level two quote are also offered on subscription from $35.00. However, you also have to pay for the bulletin board this seems a bit strong, though it may keep the loonies out.

Barchart.com**
www.barchart.com

How to use it and what for
This one is useful if you are looking to trade options, futures and commodities and need quotes for those. It is useful for the charts and analysis of those too. Given the lack of sites dealing well with derivatives data, this is a good one and the layout is pretty easy to navigate.

Although it covers stocks, don't use it for those.

Bigcharts.com***
www.bigcharts.com

How to use it and what for
Okay, if you haven't heard of this one – where *have* you been? It is one of the best charting sites around, but more of that later. We are here for quotes and quote-related features. Most online traders don't realize it is excellent for quotes because the layout is so good.

The site has the 'my favourite quotes' feature making it easier to keep tabs on your top picks – use it for that. The downside is it does not cover bulletin board stocks like Upgrade or PayforView.com. But it does allow charting straight from the quotes – dead easy to use.

BullSession.com**
www.bullsession.com

How to use it and what for
You would want to use this for its dynamic (i.e. automatic) real-time quote updating. The other key features are that you can have lots of portfolios on it and see how your profits (or maybe even your losses) look in real time. The downside – yup, there is a subscription fee. It starts at $25.95 and I would have given it three stars if it were free. However, it does provide about as much quote-related info as you could hope for for the price, including:

- bid and ask
- bid and ask size
- last trade
- close
- open

- volume
- tick
- price alerts
- daily high and low
- 52-week high and low

- price/earnings (p/e) ratios
- earnings
- ex-dividend rate
- yield
- number of trades.

Datalink***

www.datalink.net

How to use it and what for

The excellent magazine *SmartMoney* rated this service the number one alert service. The key reason to consider using this service is that it can notify you of real-time quotes and other market information on a pager. But what sane person wants to be away from their PC during market hours anyway?

Use this one also if you are a mutual fund junky.

As they explain, you are alerted via your pager or PCS phone whenever your stocks exceed the 'alert' criteria you've set. These 'alert' criteria include:

- fixed increases or decreases in the price of a stock, such as MSFT shares going up or down by more than $3.00

- relative high and low market price thresholds of a particular stock, such as MSFT exceeding a high of $145.00 or going below $105.00

- daily trading volumes for a particular stock, such as a daily volume of more than 1,000,000 shares.

When one of the stocks you are monitoring exceeds one of your set thresholds, QuoteXpress automatically sends you an alert.

eSignal***

www.esignal.com

How to use it and what for

This site is part of the Data Broadcasting Corporation, one of the most reliable names in the quote and market information industry. Use this one effectively to get top-of-the-range real-time quotes so your PC or laptop basically becomes a ticker-tape machine. As well as quotes you can, of course, get news charts and research. But you would really use this if you were going to be trading quite intensively and also wanted quotes for options and commodities. It is internet delivered and you are using eSignal because it is a reliable brand that should not have any downtime! The downside is it costs – from $79 upwards per month (although this can vary).

EuropeanInvestor.com***

www.europeaninvestor.com

How to use it and what for

The great thing about the quotes on this site is that it covers from one place every single major European market, plus the US. In the world of global online trading where more people are considering trading foreign stocks, this is a great site to get quotes – very convenient. The layout and design are also excellent.

It is a site for more than quotes, of course, including European corporate news – after all, they are based in Brussels. More of that later when we look at excellent news and research sites.

Free Real Time***

www.freerealtime.com

How to use it and what for

The site name tells you exactly what you may want to use this one for – the quotes are real time and they are free. A lot of traders still think you have to pay for online real-time quotes. This site proves you don't. It is useful and easy to use. I find it most useful when the markets are moving quickly or I am monitoring several positions, any one of which I may be looking to enter or exit imminently and so timing is of the essence. Don't use it for delayed quotes – you can get those anywhere, like on some of the other sites we are going to mention.

Interactive Investor International***

www.iii.co.uk

How to use it and what for

The quotes on iii are pretty run of the mill but the thing to use this one for is to set e-mail alerts to yourself if a stock price reaches a certain level. That way even if you are at work and can't constantly receive real-time price because of firewalls or because of company policy, you can at least still get your e-mail alert. What is even more useful is that you can set those alerts on UK and US stocks from the same single site.

Island***

www.isld.com

How to use it and what for

There are those people who know what Island is and what an ECN is. If you are one of the unlucky few who don't, then here goes – Island is an electronic communications network (ECN). Think of it as a trading network through which you can place trades, or, as they put it: 'Island is a computerized trading system that gives brokerages the power to electronically display and match stock orders for retail and institutional investors.'

Use their Top 20 list to find the quotes for the most popular stocks on their ECN and therefore which ones Island users are most focused on. This gives an indication of where the action is and what may be the most volatile stocks of the day and possibly the next few days. Of course, that leads you on to more research. Nothing on this site is enough to base an investment decision on, but you get to see close up what is happening.

You get free level II quotes to see what the demand is for a particular stock. I find this both really informative and hypnotic. They are telling you how strong the underlying demand is, albeit only on their own ECN; the quotes show you the levels at which buyers and sellers want to buy and sell and at what price and what size.

Buy orders	Sell orders	
Shares price	Shares price	Shares price
$\frac{1000}{8\frac{5}{8}}$	$\frac{200}{13\frac{1}{2}}$	$\frac{1000}{15}$
$\frac{370}{8\frac{9}{16}}$	$\frac{100}{13\frac{3}{4}}$	$\frac{125}{15\frac{1}{2}}$
	$\frac{105}{14}$	$\frac{100}{19\frac{1}{4}}$
	$\frac{100}{14}$	$\frac{1300}{21\frac{3}{8}}$
	$\frac{1000}{15}$	$\frac{500}{22}$

appendix 2

Earnings sites

The sites

Earnings Whispers**

www.earningswhispers.com

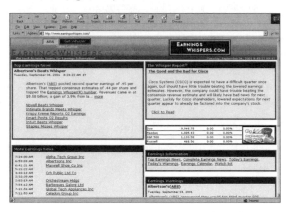

How to use it and what for

We have discussed companies meeting, exceeding or falling
below earnings expectations and some argue that it is not the
published expected earnings that matter but 'whisper numbers'
or the real figures Wall Street insiders are examining. They would
argue that that is why stock prices sometimes fall on apparently
better than expected earnings – because the figure did not meet
Street expectations. Use this site to get a handle on what the
whisper numbers are and also why they are important.

First Call**
www.firstcall.com

How to use it and what for

See the consensus change link for the most useful part of the site
for private investors. Beyond that I prefer other sites for other
earnings information. Most things are premium so really this is
for the 'heavy-duty' earnings player.

Hemmington Scott***
www.hemmscott.co.uk

How to use it and what for

The company syndicates its content to most UK online sites
providing financial information and so you may want to go
straight to the source. Its earnings and dividends link is the key
one in relation to our earlier discussion, but the site has a wealth
of other corporate information.

Market Guide***
www.marketguide.com

How to use it and what for

I have already complimented this site's excellent earnings and
other fundamental data. Use the earnings table you will find from
the home page for any company you are investing in.

Yahoo! Finance UK**

finance.uk.yahoo.com

How to use it and what for

The site improves monthly and should be used as a one-stop shop for financial information of all kinds.

Zacks Investment Research***

www.zacks.com

How to use it and what for

There are few more respected companies on the web. Use the free services for earnings data. There are subscription services too for much more such as e-mail portfolio earnings updates. Use the one-month free trial. The site is particularly useful if you are looking for free earnings surprise information.

Fundamental data

The sites

Bloomberg***
www.bloomberg.com; www.bloomberg.co.uk

How to use it and what for
A wealth of analysis of fundamental data as they hit the news screens. Get intelligent analysis here first.

FTMarketwatch.com***
www.ftmarketwatch.com

How to use it and what for
Again, what does that earnings report mean? Why is the price moving? The columnists here take a thoughtful approach to get behind figures and market-moving stories.

Hoover's***

www.hoovers.com

How to use it and what for

This one also covers, mainly for subscriptions, many types of information we have looked at so far, including proprietary company profiles which are syndicated to some other financial portals.

Insider Trading**

www.insidertrader.com

How to use it and what for

If you liked the ideas discussed earlier about insider trading then this is the one for you. The site collates in one useful place the key insider buying and selling of corporate executives.

Market Guide***

www.marketguide.com

How to use it and what for

See Chapter 7 for my take on this site.

Multex Investor Network***

www.multexinvestor.com

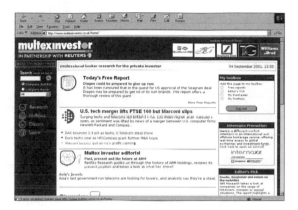

How to use it and what for

This site has a multitude of broker research reports ranging from
the free to the very expensive. I tend to focus on the free ones since
I am an active trader. Longer term investors may want to invest in
a report to back up their trading decisions.

Brokers

Broker watch

In this appendix we take a run through sites that rate and rank brokers according to different criteria such as performance, speed, commissions etc.

Ameritrade***
www.ameritrade.com

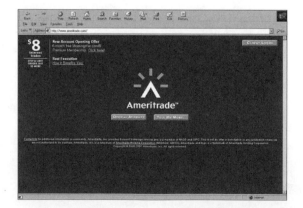

How to use it and what for

A very good site. The home page is a lesson in simplicity coupled
with professionalism. The site is quick; research is not as good as
others but then again the broker is one of the cheapest around.
Very easy to navigate and designed very well with less clutter
than other sites.

Charles Schwab***
www.eschwab.com

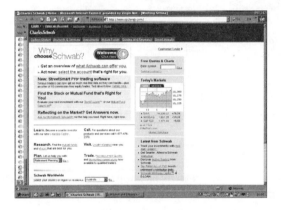

How to use it and what for

Charles Schwab is not the cheapest broker but it doesn't care
because it is the largest. Very experienced at what it does and has
an enormous number of positive press comments. If you are a
little concerned about trading on the net then a broker such as
Schwab provides some added security in that you are dealing
with an old hand in internet broking. I wish they would use their
size to do even more strategic alliances and offer their clients even
more free stuff, however.

Charles Schwab Europe***

www.schwab-worldwide.com/worldwide/europe;
www.sharelink.com

How to use it and what for

An increasingly impressive site, with free research, easy naviga-
bility and good design. There is also a phone brokerage service for
those not quite ready to jump on to the cybertrain. Also offers UK
investors the opportunity to buy US securities.

Datek***

www.datek.com

How to use it and what for

Not only is Datek cheap, but I do keep on hearing good things about it from chat boards, e-mails and press comment. Either it has a very good CIA like undercover publicity machine or it is, in fact, very good. The site also has a reassuring number of positive press reviews. I always find that comforting when considering a site marketing itself on the basis of having a very low cost base.

Discover**
www.discoverbrokerage.com

How to use it and what for
Owned by Morgan Stanley, but the site does not come in as having the lowest commission, the best design or the most research. It sort of does a bit of everything without excelling at all or indeed any one. However, given who owns it, it provides the security you may want in an online broker.

DLJ Direct**
www.dljdirect.com

How to use it and what for
The US site is very nice and well organized. It gives you reasons to open an account and makes it easy to find commission rates. DLJ realizes it has to offer added value through research and does so. The only thing is that it is not the very cheapest.

DLJ Direct UK***

www.dljdirect.co.uk

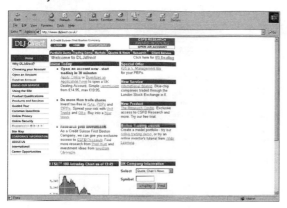

How to use it and what for

A relatively new entrant to the UK market; the site is well constructed with good research available. It is fast and slick. Liked it.

E*Trade***
www.etrade.com

How to use it and what for

A site with a lot of features, some free before you register, others for account holders. The site is easy to navigate and the information is very easy to find. On the Gomez rankings they have been the Number 1 overall broker for some time. As brokers, they have a lot of awards and positive reviews making them a must-consider broker.

Message boards and financial services are also available from the site.

E*Trade UK**

www.etrade.co.uk

How to use it and what for

The UK version of the US site is among the very best of all the sites
open to UK investors. The charting section is especially good.
Offers portfolios, message boards (which could be better
organized but are among the most active in the UK for stock chat),
news and research. Well designed and organized. Did I mention
that the commissions are among the UK's lowest?

Gomez***

www.gomez.com

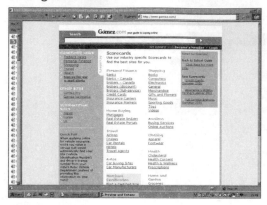

How to use it and what for

Use this excellent site to see how online brokers rank based on different criteria such as cost, customer service, resources and 'overall'.

Internet Investing**

www.internetinvesting.com

How to use it and what for

Use this one for more specific details on the commission rates and minimum account sizes plus account information about main c brokers. A bit textual rather than tabular and slightly semi-professional in look.

Keynote Web Brokerage Index**
www.keynote.com

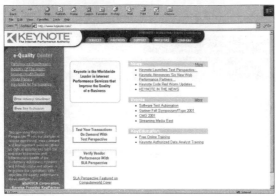

How to use it and what for
Use this for an intriguing look at which e-brokers' sites are the fastest for access; useful when time is of the essence for short-term active traders.

Merrill Lynch HSBC***
www.mlhsbc.com

How to use it and what for
Broker that offers integrated cash, savings and investment accounts in the UK, Australia and Canada for Merrill Lynch's mass affluents. Offers good news educational services and an excellent client service through prominently located investment centres. A reputable global broker and one of the only to offer investors Airmiles.

Pathburner***
www.pathburner.com

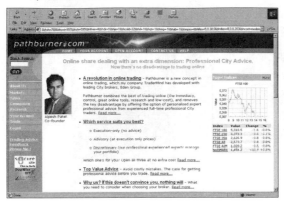

How to use it and what for
Taking online broking to the next level for those who don't want
to make their own decisions or want a second opinion, this broker
offers professional advice at execution-only discount prices from
a well-respected parent firm.

Scottrade**
www.scottrade.com

How to use it and what for

The site seems to be extremely slow. It is supposed to be cheap, however, and I liked the design and layout of the site.

Smart Money Broker Ratings***

www.smartmoney.com

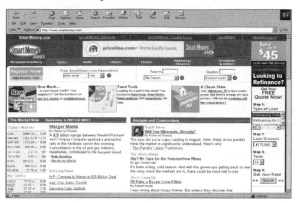

How to use it and what for

An excellent site and magazine. Use this site for things like the seductive broker speedometer. The site has brokers ranked by lots of criteria. It is a great lesson in how to present information too.

Xest**

www.xest.com

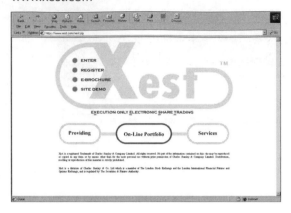

How to use it and what for

A much improved site, but still needs some improvement to assist download speeds. Some of the graphics did not seem to download and knowing where to start or open an account was not as easy as on some other sites. Seems to have been designed by IT specialists without consultation with an online trader.

Technical analysis sites

Bigcharts***
www.bigdiagrams.com

How to use it and what for

The quick diagram function is straightforward. It draws the diagram quickly, but that is not why we want to use this site. You can get diagrams anywhere – we want the good stuff from the best people. That is where the free Interactive Charting button comes in. Use that for comparison of stock performances to other stocks, to indices, to plot indicators.

It is particularly useful because you can choose the indicators and can have more than one.

Note: ClearStation limits you on the former and Equis limits you on the latter.

Equis**
www.equis.com

How to use it and what for

The best thing about this site, other than as a place from which to buy the excellent Metastock software is the interactive charting part of the site. Again, most people do not realize it exists because it is a little hidden away but click on Online Charting to get to it.

Use it for a more sophisticated charting package than at ClearStation; you can zoom in and out very easily, plot Japanese candlestick diagrams, plot more technical indicators and plot trendlines. All this for free.

Trading Charts*

www.tradingcharts.com

How to use it and what for

Use this if you really don't want all the complex technical analysis stuff cluttering up your screen and you are looking for a crisp, clean, easy-to-see diagram for simplicity's sake. It is best suited to a fundamental analyst who wants to look at diagrams.

The MyDiagrams function is really useful for storing the stocks for which you are regularly going to want to see the diagrams. It would be even better if you could scroll from one to the next, but it is still helpful.

Other good sites you are likely to come across

In this section I want briefly to run down my view on some other charting sites that you may come across but which I am not necessarily recommending for regular use – I feel those already listed do the job better or are more comprehensive. However, here's my opinion on some of the rest.

Barchart
www.barchart.com

How to use it and what for
Mostly free, but some tools do cost. Well designed and good value for money. Has all the basics you would need and good for more advanced stuff too.

DecisionPoint
www.decisionpoint.com

How to use it and what for
DecisionPoint offers extensive technical analysis charting functions and indicators as well as historical diagrams. All for a fee.

My view is that I don't want to pay for these things if a lot of them can be found free elsewhere. Also, if I am into the really heavy-duty technical indicators why not just buy software such as Superdiagrams?

E*Trade UK**

www.etrade.co.uk

How to use it and what for

I told you I would try to find the hidden gems. If you are looking for diagrams on UK equities and want indicators such as momentum and comparison of securities' performances plus easy educational material on how to interpret all this, then this is the place for you.

IDQ

www.siliconinvestor.com

How to use it and what for

IQC is a great little site – now part of Silicon Investor – but again the same story; I won't pay for something I can get from software or free sites already recommended in this book.

Interactive Investor International
www.iii.co.uk

How to use it and what for
Although this site gets a lot of publicity due to its marketing effort after flotation, its strong point is not its charting, which could be improved.

MarketEdge
www.stkwtch.com

How to use it and what for
Other than the stupid web address, this is not too bad. You would use it if you want to pay for quite detailed stock picks based on technical analysis from an experienced money manager. I prefer my own research – maybe I am too cocky or just too cheap to pay for someone else's advice!

Wright Research Center**

www.profiles.wisi.com

How to use it and what for

This site is useful for finding diagrams of stocks of different countries all from the same site. If you are a fundamental analyst you will like this too because as well as the diagram it gives a host of fundamental data about the stock on the same page, but what I really like is that it plots earnings and dividends on the same diagram so you can see how they are doing too.

Use this to judge any company whose stock prices seem to be taking off relative to their earnings; it may be a quick visual guide to overvaluation. Diagram A5.1 shows how earnings (represented by the top line) have not been increasing at the same rate as the stock price. While that is not a buy or sell signal, it puts you on notice that the company will have to make great strides to meet the expectations that have built up in the company.

It would be even better if it plotted EPS or p/e and PEG ratios too.

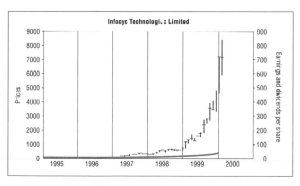

DIAGRAM A5.1 ■ Great strides to meet great expectations?

Glossary

Abandoned option   Where an option is neither sold nor exercised but allowed to lapse at expiry.

Accumulation   A technical analysis term describing a stock whose price is moving sideways.

Acid test ratio   A measure of financial strength. Also known as the quick ratio. Cash plus short-term investments plus accounts receivable divided by current liabilities for the same period. All other things being equal, a relatively high figure should indicate a healthy company.

Active channels   A feature of Internet Explorer 4. Internet sites that are selected as channels provide special IE4 content. Gates wants to lead internet tv – hence the term channels.

Active market   Securities trading with a relatively high degree of liquidity, the major benefit of which is narrow spreads. A term of art rather then precision.

Aftermarket   Also known as 'secondary market', refering to the trading in a security after its initial public offering.

All or none   Order instructing the broker to buy or sell the entire amount of the order in one transaction or not at all.

American depositary receipt (ADR)   Effectively like owning in dollars stocks of non-US-listed companies. A popular form of owning shares of foreign companies.

American option   An option that is exerciseable at any time within its life. May be traded outside Europe and are.

American Stock Exchange (AMEX)   Located in New York, this is the third-largest US stock exchange. Shares trade in the same 'auction' manner used by the larger New York Stock Exchange unlike the NASDAQ's 'market-making' methods.

Arbitrage   The purchase in one market of an instrument and the sale in another market of it or a closely linked instrument in order to profit from the small price differentials between the products in the two markets. Arbitrage profits usually only exist for a small time because someone usually scoops on them since they are 'locked in'.

Arbitrageur   A trader engaged in arbitrage. They seek to make a lot of small, quick profits.

Ask   The lowest price at which a dealer or market maker will sell a security (also, 'bid', 'offer').

Assign   To oblige a call option writer to sell shares to the option holder or to oblige a put option writer to buy shares from a put option holder.

At the close   Order instructing to be filled as close as possible to the, um, close of a particular security, or to be cancelled otherwise.

At the market   An order to buy or sell at the best price obtainable in the market.

At the open   Order instructing the transaction to be filled in one of the first trades for a particular security or to be cancelled otherwise.

Averaging   Where a price moves against a trader and he trades more of the stock to enlarge his position but to lower his overall entry price. It will mean he will have a lower exit price at which he can make a profit.

Away from the market   Trade orders that cannot be executed because they are above or below the current bid or ask. For example, a limit order to buy 50 shares of AOL at $105 when the best offer is $109 will not be filled and is said to be 'away from the market'.

Backbone   A high-speed connection within a network that connects all the other circuits. Another name for a 'hub'. A central connection from which 'spokes' or connections radiate.

Bandwidth   The capacity of a network to carry data. If your pipes are clogged (low bandwidth) then things take forever to load. It's an issue not of length but of width.

Basis point   Used to calculate differences in interest rate yields, e.g. the difference between 5.25 percent and 6.00 percent is 75 basis points.

BBS   A bulletin board system. A little like an electronic notice board. You 'post' messages to the board and everyone who subscribes to the board can view them.

Bear(ish)   An individual who thinks prices will fall.

Bear market   A market in which prices are falling.

Bear spread   An option position where it is intended to profit from a falling market. Usually the position involves the purchase of a put at one strike price and the sale of a put at a lower strike price.

Beta   This measures the stock's volatility to the market as a whole. A beta value greater than 1.0 represents greater volatility than the general market; less than 1.0 represents less volatility than the general market.

Bid   An offer to purchase at a specific price.

Big Board   Nickname for the New York Stock Exchange. Greatly adds to your smugability if you only ever refer to the NYSE as the Big Board. The ignorant will instantly fall admiringly at your feet. That a person of flesh and blood could know so much!?

Black–Scholes Pricing Modelability   A mathematical model used to calculate the price in theory of an option. The main input variables are: the risk-free interest rate, volatility, dividends, time to expiry, the strike price, underlying price.

Block   As in 'the sale of a block of shares'. A transaction involving a large number of shares or other security. Often blocks are bought or sold at a discount to the current market as an accepted cost of trading a large number of shares.

Boiler room   Derogatory term to describe a brokerage firm where investors are aggressively solicited over the telephone with high-pressure telephone sales tactics. Smug traders, stay well clear.

Bounce   What happens to mail which for some reason (e.g. wrong e-mail address) cannot be delivered.

Breadth   Comparison of issues traded on a stock exchange on a given day to the total number of issues listed for trading. The broader a market move the more significant it is.

Break   A sudden fall in price.

Breakout   When the price moves out of its recent range. Sometimes signals further moves in the direction of the breakout.

Broker   An individual who executes customers' orders.

Bucket shop   Slang term for a disreputable brokerage firm that regularly engages in illegal practices, such as selling customers stock it may own at a higher than market price without disclosing the fact.

Bull(ish)   An individual who believes prices will rise.

Bull market   A market in which prices are rising.

Bull spread   An option position where it is intended to profit from a rising market. Usually the position involves the purchase of a call at one strike price and the sale of a call at a higher strike price.

Buy in   A person having to buy a security because of an inability to deliver the shares from a previous sale of said shares. Often associated with short sellers.

Call option (calls)   The right, but not the obligation, existing only for a fixed period of time, to purchase a fixed quantity of stock at a fixed price.

Cash flow per share   The trailing 12-month cash flow divided by the 12-month average shares outstanding. All other things being equal, a relatively high figure, growing steadily, is sign of a growing and healthy company and may indicate a rising share price.

Churning   Illegal practice by a broker to cause excessive transactions in a client's account to benefit the broker through increased transaction fees.

Clerk   An employee of an exchange's member firm, who is registered to work on the exchange floor.

Closed   When referring to a position this means one has made an equal and opposite trade to one already held and so has no more exposure to the market on that trade.

Co-mingling   Illegal act of combining client assets with those of the brokerage to boost the fiduciary's financial standing.

Contrarian   An individual who generally believes it is usually better not to do what the majority is doing, because the majority does not make money.

Cookie   According to conspiracy theorists, a cookie is a small piece of software that is downloaded from a website to your computer's hard drive that tells the web master all your hidden and deepest secrets. According to everyone else, a cookie is a small piece of software that is downloaded from a website to your computer's hard drive that tells the web master your username, password, viewing preference and one or two other things. It means you do not have to enter the same information over and over again.

Crossed market   The highest bid is greater than the lowest offer due to buyer and seller imbalance. Usually only lasts a few seconds until the market 'sorts itself out'.

Current ratio   The ratio of total current assets divided by the total current liabilities for the same period. A measure of financial strength. All other things being equal, a relatively high figure would indicate a healthy company.

Cyberspace   William Gibson's name in his fantasy novel *Neuromancer* (William Gibson, 1994) to describe what is now known as the internet.

Daisy chain   Creating the illusion of trading activity in a stock through collusion of a number of brokers. Yes, it is illegal.

Day trade(r)   A position that is closed the same day it was opened.

Deep discount   Often, internet brokers that charges commissions far less than full service or discount brokers; as cheap as you can get.

Delta   The change of the options price for a change in the underlying price. A delta of 0.5 means a ten-point move in the underlying causes a five-point move in the option.

Depreciation   Not a measure of spousal dissatisfaction. An accounting measure used to reduce the value of capital expenditure for the purposes of reclaiming tax.

Diversification   Reducing risk by spreading investments among different interments. Not putting all your eggs in a few baskets.

Dividend ex-date   This is the date from which a purchaser of the stock will not be entitled to receive the last announced dividend. Appropriately, when a stock goes ex-dividend its price falls by approximately the value of the dividend.

Dividend growth rate   A measure of corporate growth. The annual positive change in dividend paid to stockholders. All other things being equal, an increase should indicate a growing company and should be reflected in rising share price.

Dividend rate   This is the total expected dividends for the forthcoming 12 months. It is usually the value of the most recent dividend figure multiplied by the number of times dividends are paid in a year, plus any extra dividend payments.

Dividend yield   This is calculated by dividing the annual dividend by the current price and expressing the figure as a percentage.

Domain   Part of a web or e-mail address. Separated from the rest of the address by dots.

Dotted quad   A set of four numbers separated by dots that constitutes an internet address, e.g. 123.32.433.234.

Down tick   A trade in a security that was executed at a lower price than the previous trade; same as 'minus tick'.

EPS   Earnings per share. A measure of corporate growth. The value of corporate earning divided by the number of shares outstanding. All other things being equal, a growing figure reflects a healthy growing company and should be reflected in the share price.

European option   An option that is only exercisable at expiry.

Exercise   Where the holder of an option uses his right to buy or sell the underlying security. Also means to workout.

Expiry   The date up to which a trader can exercise his option.

Flame   An e-mail that is abusive or argumentative. Usually includes the words 'You are a …' somewhere in the message.

Flamefest   The same as a flame orgy.

Flat   (1) A market where the price of a stock and/or its volume have/has not changed significantly over a period of time; (2) no longer to hold a position in a particular security or account.

Floor broker   A member who executes orders for clearing members.

Floor trader   An individual who trades on the floor of an exchange either for himself or a company.

Free speech   An issue relating to the internet about which the US Congress spends inordinate quantities of time. Essentially, the concern is to give rights to those who would deny them to others, including those who granted them.

Freeriding   Rapid buying and selling of a security by a broker without putting up funds for the purchase. Yup, it is illegal.

Front running   Buying or selling securities ahead of a large order so as to benefit from the subsequent price move.

FTP   (file transfer protocol) The protocol for sending files through the internet.

Fundamental analysis   Forecasting prices by using economic or accounting data. For example, one might base a decision to buy a stock on its yield.

Futures   A standardized contract for the future delivery of goods, at a pre-arranged date, location, price.

Gap   Where a price opens and trades higher than its previous close.

Geek   Also known as a net nerd. They were the kids everyone hated at school, who wore thick black-rimmed spectacles and were extremely uncool. They would also get sand kicked in their faces and were so unpopular no one would be seen dead with them – sometimes not even their parents. Now the sand has settled and it has become clear that because they were unpopular they spent all their time studying, and can now be considered some of the wealthiest people on the planet, with the fastest, flashiest cars. They definitely had the last laugh.

Gross margin   A measure of company profitability. The previous 12-month total revenue less cost of goods sold divided by the total revenue. All other things being equal, a decrease in gross margins could indicate troubled times ahead.

Hedge   Protection against current or anticipated risk exposure, usually through the purchase of a derivative. For example, if you hold DM and fear that the price will decline in relation to the dollar you may go long dollar. You would then make some profit on your long position to offset your losses in holding DM.

Hit the bid   When a seller places market orders with the intention of selling to the highest bidder, regardless of price.

Implied volatility   Future price volatility as calculated from actual, not theoretical, options prices. The volatility is implied in the prices.

In and out   Term for day trading in a security.

Income per employee   The income after taxes divided by the number of employees. A measure of corporate efficiency. All other things being equal, a greater the figure or a growing figure indicates a more efficient company and should be reflected in a rising share price.

Initial margin requirement   Amount of cash and securities a customer must have in his/her account before trading on margin.

Initial public offering (IPO)   First sale of stock by a company to the public.

Insider   Person such as a corporate officer or director with access to privileged company information.

Insider share purchases   The number of shares in the company purchased by its insiders – officers and directors – over a stated period of time. All other things being equal, a relatively large move may indicate a forthcoming upward move in the stock price.

INSTINET   A 'fourth stock market' allowing members to display bid and ask quotes and bypass brokers in securities transactions. Owned by Reuters.

Institutional net shares purchased   This is the difference between institutional share purchases less institutional share sales in the company over a stated period of time. All other things being equal, a relatively large move may indicate a forthcoming upward move in the stock price.

Institutional percent owned   This is the percentage of shares owned by all the institutions taken together. It is a percentage of the total shares outstanding. All other things being equal, a relatively large move may indicate a forthcoming upward move in the stock price.

Intranet   This is a collection of computers connected to one another, usually located in a company or other organization. Unlike the internet, the network is private and not principally intended for the public.

Java   An island or a coffee bean or a programming language developed by Sun Microsystems. It allows users to do lots of clever things with web pages.

LAN (local area network)   A network of computers operating up to a few thousand metres from each other.

Level I quotes   Basic service of the NASDAQ stock market that displays current bid and ask quotes.

Level II quotes   Service of the NASDAQ stock market that displays current bid and ask quotes and the bids and asks from all market makers in a particular stock.

Level III quotes   Service of the NASDAQ stock market that allows a market maker or registered broker–dealer to enter a bid or ask on the electronic trading system.

Limit   The maximum permitted price move up or down for any given day, under exchange rules.

Liquid market   A market which permits relatively easy entry and exit of large orders because there are so many buyers and sellers. Usually a characteristic of a popular market.

Long   A position, opened but not yet closed, with a buy order.

Long-term debt to total equity   A measure of financial strength. The long-term debt of the company divided by the total shareholder equity for the same period. All other things being equal, a relatively high figure may indicate an unhealthy company.

Margin   A sum placed with a broker by a trader to cover against possible losses.

Margin call   A demand for cash to maintain margin requirements.

Mark to market   Daily calculation of paper gains and losses using closing market prices. Also used to calculate any necessary margin that may be payable.

Market capitalization   This is the product of the number of shares outstanding and the current price.

Market order   *see* At the market

MIME   Multipurpose internet mail extensions. This enables you to attach files to e-mail.

Momentum   An indicator used by traders to buy or sell. It is based on the theory that the faster and further prices move in a particular direction, the more likely they are to slow and turn.

Moving average   A system used by traders to determine when to buy and sell. An average (simple, exponential or other) is taken of the closing (or opening or other) prices over a specific number of previous days. A plot is made based on the average. As each day progresses, the moving average has to be recalculated to take account of the latest data and remove the oldest data.

Net   After expenses or short for the internet.

Net profit margin   A measure of profitability. Income after taxes divided by the total revenue for the same period. All other things being equal, downward pressure on the net profit margin could provide advance warning of impending share price decline.

Netiquette   Proper net behaviour. For instance, swearing is not appropriate etiquette neither is it netiquette.

Network   A group of computers connected to each other so that their users can access each others' machines.

Offer   A price at which a seller is willing to sell.

Off-line browser   A browser that permits viewing of sites previously downloaded without being connected to the net.

Open position   A position that has not yet been closed and therefore the trader is exposed to market movements.

Overbought/oversold   A term used to mean, broadly, that a stock is likely not to advance further and may decline (overbought) or advance (oversold).

Position   Trades which result in exposure to market movements.

Price, 52-week high   This is the highest price the stock traded in the last 52 weeks. It may not necessarily be a closing high, it could be an intra-day high.

Price, 52-week low   This is the lowest price the stock traded in the past 52 weeks. Could be an intra-day low price.

Price to book ratio   The current price divided by the latest quarterly book value per share. All other things being equal, a relatively low figure may indicate the stock is undervalued.

Price to cash flow ratio   The current price divided by the cash flow per share for the trailing 12 months. All other things being equal, a relatively low figure may indicate the stock is undervalued.

Price to earnings ratio   The current share price divided by earnings per share before extraordinary items, usually taken over the previous 12 months. All other things being equal, a relatively low figure may indicate the stock is undervalued.

Protocols   A set of rules with which two computers must comply in order to communicate.

Push technology   The internet can be quite a passive experience, needing the user to log onto a site to determine if changes have occurred or to download information. With push technology, the browser can be set automatically to download data from a set site.

Put option   A right, but not the obligation, existing for a specified period of time, to sell a specific quantity of stock or other instrument at a specified price.

Pyramiding   The increase in size of an existing position by opening further positions, usually in decreasing increments.

Quick ratio   A measure of financial strength. Cash plus short term investments plus accounts receivable divided by current liabilities for the same period. All other things being equal, a relatively high figure may indicate a healthy company. *See also* Acid test ratio

Return on assets   A measure of management effectiveness. Income after taxes divided by the total assets. All other things being equal, a relatively high or growing figure may indicate a company doing well.

Return on equity   A measure of management effectiveness. Income available to shareholders divided by the total common equity. All other things being equal, a relatively high or growing figure may indicate a company doing well.

Return on investments   A measure of management effectiveness. Income after taxes divided by the average total assets long-term debt. All other things being equal, a relatively high or growing figure may indicate a company doing well.

Revenue percent change year on year   A measure of growth. The revenue of the most recent period less the revenue of the previous period divided by the revenue of the previous period. All other things being equal, a growing figure indicates a growing company and should be reflected in a rising share price.

Sales per employee   A measure of company efficiency. The total sales divided by the total number of full-time employees. All other things being equal, the greater this figure the more efficient the company.

Sales percent change   A measure of corporate growth. The value of sales for the current period less the value of sales for the preceding period divided by the value of sales for the preceding period, expressed as a percentage. All other things being equal, a growing figure indicates a growing company and should be reflected in a rising share price.

Scalper   A trader also seeks to enter and exit the market very quickly and thereby make a lot of small profits.

Seat   Exchange membership that permits floor trading.

Server   A computer that shares its resources with others. The resources may be disk space, files or something else.

Shares outstanding   The number of shares issued less those held in treasury.

Short   An open position created by a sell order, in the expectation of a price decline and so the opportunity to profit by purchasing the instrument (so 'closing out') at a lower price.

Short-term debt   The value of debt due in the next 12 months.

SMTP   (simple mail transfer protocol) The standard set of rules for transferring e-mail messages from one computer to another.

Speculator   An individual who purchases financial instruments in order to profit. Often used to refer to a non-professional. Sometimes used derogatorily.

Spread   The simultaneous purchase of one contract and the sale of a similar, but not identical, contract. Depending on the exact combination, a profit can be made from either a rising or falling market.

Stop order (stop loss orders)   An order left with a broker instructing him to close out an existing position if the market price reaches a certain level. Can be used to take profits or stop losses.

TCP/IP   (transmission control protocol/internet protocol) A set of rules used to connect to other computers.

Technical analysis   Method used to forecast future prices using the price data alone (for example, by plotting them on a chart and noting direction) or using the price as an input in mathematical formulae and plotting the results. *See also* Fundamental analysis

Technical rally or decline   A price movement resulting from factors unrelated to fundamentals or supply and demand.

Tick   The smallest possible price move.

Total debt to equity ratio   A measure of financial strength. The total debt divided by total shareholder equity for the same period. All other things being equal, a relatively low figure is a sign of a healthy company.

Total operating expenses   A measure of the cost of running the company. All other things being equal, a lower figure is preferable to a higher one.

Trendline   A line on a price chart indicating market price direction. The line connects at least three price points which touch the line, with no prices breaking the line.

Volatility   A statistical indication of probable future price movement size (but not direction) within a period of time. For example 66 percent probability of a 15p move in three months.

Webcasting   This is the internet trying to be older – like tv or radio. Instead of viewing pages, you view a stream of data in the form of radio or video. Unfortunately, the infrastructure is lacking to make this a popular alternative to tv and radio.

Whipsaw   A price move first in one direction, and, shortly thereafter, in another direction thereby catching traders wrong-footed. Such markets may be termed 'choppy'. Such effects often give rise to false buy and sell signals, leading to losses.

TRADING ONLINE
Alpesh Patel

ISBN: 0273 650416

"Read the book, jump aboard the cyber-train and become a better investor." – Guy Knight, Vice President, Charles Schwab Europe

"The best guide available on how to use the Internet to improve investing performance and reduce costs." – *Internet Investor*

"You have two choices, buy this book or attend a $5000 course on cyber-trading. I'd take the former." – Neal T Weintraub, Floor Trader and author of *Tricks of the Floor Trader*

"Trading Online offers the most comprehensive and for ward-thinking guide on how to deal in the new millennium world markets." – Jack Wigglesworth, former Chairman, LIFFE

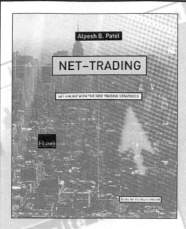

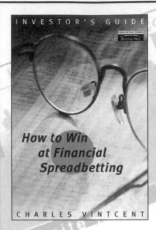

More power to your
[business-mind]

Even at the end there's more we can learn. More that we can learn from your experience of this book, and more ways to add to your learning experience.

For who to read, what to know and where to go in the world of business, visit us at **business-minds.com**.

Here you can find out more about the people and ideas that can make you and your business more innovative and productive. Each month our e-newsletter, Business-minds Express, delivers an infusion of thought leadership, guru interviews, new business practice and reviews of key business resources directly to you. Subscribe for free at

● **www.business-minds.com/goto/newsletters**

Here you can also connect with ways of putting these ideas to work. Spreading knowledge is a great way to improve performance and enhance business relationships. If you found this book useful, then so might your colleagues or customers. If you would like to explore corporate purchases or custom editions personalised with your brand or message, then just get in touch at

● **www.business-minds.com/corporatesales**

We're also keen to learn from your experience of our business books – so tell us what you think of this book and what's on your business mind with an online reader report at business-minds.com. Together with our authors, we'd like to hear more from you and explore new ways to help make these ideas work at

● **www.business-minds.com/goto/feedback**

[www.business-minds.com
www.financialminds.com]